Stuck Entrepreneurs

Stuck Entrepreneurs

Escape Routes Out of the Quicksand

Jay J. Silverberg

BEP

BUSINESS EXPERT PRESS

Leader in applied, concise business books

First published in 2023 by
Business Expert Press, LLC
222 East 46th Street, New York, NY 10017
www.businessexpertpress.com

ISBN-13: 978-1-63742-432-2 (paperback)
ISBN-13: 978-1-63742-433-9 (e-book)

Business Expert Press Entrepreneurship and Small Business Management Collection

First edition: 2023

10 9 8 7 6 5 4 3 2 1

Entrepreneurship is an art that requires great creativity and innovative thinking, a science that requires developing skills and reasoning, and a high pain threshold for when things go bump in the night, and they often do.

On a personal note, this book is meant to inspire, forewarn, teach and entertain, and hopefully not mess you up too much. For certain, it will make you a better, free-thinking, less stuck entrepreneur.

Thank you to my wife, Linda, and my other sounding boards;- my children Lauren, Noah and Jonathan. They know when to inflate and deflate me, and keep me focused.

Thanks as well to Bruce McLean and Lex Dunn for their friendship and content contributions.

Description

Learn to Escape, Avoid or Sidestep Your Descent into the Quicksand

Stuck Entrepreneurs provides inventive strategies for the quicksand mired businessperson who asks *what am I doing wrong?* or *how can I break this inertia and move my business forward?* It provides keen, often uncommon lessons in breakout entrepreneurship.

Whatever stage of your business journey you find yourself stuck in; the author delivers advice that is steeped in real-world experience gleaned from his own variety of business ventures.

Stuck Entrepreneurs casts a wide target readership net; from academia (business students and university professors), and wanna-be or early stage entrepreneurs seeking a foothold for their ventures, to established businesses floundering in the paralysis of quicksand.

Stuck Entrepreneurs is packed with the author's business stories. Some are happy; others are, well, disturbing. But they all deliver precious guidance; the creative fodder that keeps vigilant entrepreneurs in the game.

Most importantly, *Stuck Entrepreneurs* is a **combination business manual and a workbook**. Each chapter includes a challenging, self-directed workbook to encourage the reader to learn from the best counsel I can offer.

Together, the manual and workbook are designed to extract you out of the quicksand, dust off your duds, steady your business gait, and put you back on your entrepreneurial journey, heading in the right direction.

Jay Silverberg is not a book writer who calls himself an entrepreneur. He is a successful entrepreneur who wrote this book as part of a three-volume collection to get other entrepreneurs like you out of the quicksand.

He is not a "pretend" business guru who practices what he calls "guru-cide," that is, those who deliver unactionable, stale, and clichéd advice, and "you can do it—rah rah cheerleading." He is the real-deal with the laurels and wounds to prove it.

And, yes, he has also taken some hits along the way. Who hasn't? You get the benefit of his experience. He is not shy to share his scars. Everything is a "how to" or "how not to" learning experience.

You're welcome.

Keywords

entrepreneurship; stuck; escape the quicksand; pivot; real world business advice; avoid the quicksand; rebirth; business pitfalls; reframing business; survival; post-Covid business; business problems; business stories; overcoming business adversity; business adventures; business games; slipping into quicksand

Contents

Prologue

Don't Play Where You Don't Belong

For a short while I did business in Russia, until the Capone-style mafia decided I was a fair target for extortion, and I decided I wanted to enjoy my golden years.

One of my ventures was importing consumer goods from Scandinavia into Moscow via St Petersburg. These consisted of decent clothing, kitchen supplies, and health care products. Nothing terribly exciting but all in short supply in Russia. Sounds pretty safe, right?

My first test shipment of three truckloads went very smoothly and produced a decent profit. I was now pumped, confident beyond reason, greedy and reckless beyond cautious.

I upped the stakes.

My next shipment consisted of a 25-truck convoy packed with kitchenware. It was stopped no less than 17 times, at gunpoint, by mafioso overlords who extracted bribes to let the trucks pass. Slowly the trucks emptied as tolls were collected in kind. It seemed that the Russian mafia was regionalized, almost franchised, and likely the best organized infrastructure in all of Russia.

I kept receiving phone calls from Ivan, the convoy lead driver. Seventeen calls in all, each increasing in urgency. Realizing that I had zero control and was way beyond my comfort zone, my only advice was that before the next extortion stop, he repack the trucks so that the cheap goods were at the back, easy to unload by the McMafia.

By the time my trucks, or what was left of them, arrived in Moscow, all I had left were two cases of dishcloths and a shaken collection of drivers anxious to be paid.

My Russian misadventure came to a quick end. I headed home to safety having learned the harsh lesson not to play where I didn't belong.

And never again to let the excitement (and avarice) of the opportunity eclipse my need to do my homework before I dive in.

I left the dishcloths in Mother Russia.

Glossary of Terms

A preapology. In writing this book, I seem to have been inspired to expand upon the meaning of certain words in the English language as applied specifically to business. This also included the need to invent new terms when I found myself "stuckified." Further apologies to Noah Webster.

Quicksand: Arriving at, approaching, or being drawn toward, unknowingly or inadvertently, a place in time and space where you will experience difficulties in your business; your focus will be drawn away from the normal operations of your business; extrication will prove difficult; generally a negative impact on your venture; a warning that things need to change, or issues and challenges need to be resolved; often creates or exacerbates personal issues that parallel business challenges.

Quicksand Pit: A place where you are experiencing immobility of action and reaction to challenges; a situation that calls for immediate business remedial action; an awakening to the problems at hand; a call to action.

Stuck: An inability to move or take corrective action; adherence to character or performance shortcomings or flaws that can or have impacted on your business; rejecting change; stubbornness; no clear pathway of change; uncertainty in your decision making; "turning a blind eye"; unwillingness to face pending or existing threats.

Stuckicide: A place where you are stuck, with a narrowing perspective on how to initiate change or take corrective action; placing yourself in danger by virtue of not recognizing that you are stuck, or about to be stuck.

Stuckified: The act of getting stuck.

Stuckhood: The unfortunate place where you have landed; the "hood"' of stuck.

Guru: Generally refers to a "know it all" with limited hands-on experience in what they are professing; a derogatory term; the ability to spout generalities that pass as counsel; purveyors of nonrealizable advice; often out-of-touch with your actual needs; deliver programs that do not change with changing market and business environment times; self-professed experts.

Gurucide: The delivery of advice by gurus that can often have detrimental impact on your business; generic; business mentoring and counselling that is limited in its usefulness; not helpful; having been drawn in by the possibilities of help; empty promises.

Edgy: Being different or acting differently, often beyond the norm, for example, guerilla-type marketing; making an intended impression; being intentionally memorable, referring to a person, brand or marketing strategy/campaign; the ability to stand out, but in a good way; acting out in order to be recognized.

Social Moodia: Where you can gage the marketplace by reading Pam's posting of where and what she ate, who she is seeing romantically and why her friends hate her; pestering on a medium where everyone is mostly selling to each other; a congregation of other time-wasters; a place to post your important blog that visitors will spend under five seconds reading; a bazaar of trivia.

The Stuck Entrepreneur's School of Thinking

I often work with distraught entrepreneurs, baffled and listless to varying degrees. Because I have lived it all, those floundering stuck entrepreneurs are, well, my kind of people.

But there is hope for the stranded businessperson; solutions, safeguards, warning bells, and lifelines to extricate you from the quicksand. That is what "Stuck Entrepreneurs" delivers.

We all go into business with the highest of expectations and, often, with a preconception that we can do it. Of course we can; this kind of mindset is part of the entrepreneurial starry dream.

We know others who have been successful. We read about them, drool over them. The successful role models all-too-often boast about how they made it. What they often downplay are the quicksand traps they almost succumbed to along their journey.

Quicksand awaits us all. The tough part is not being engulfed, mumbling "I should have done something earlier on."

But let's backtrack.

1. You are dreaming of a business. You have done your homework, and you believe what you want to believe, and ignore the red flags. They don't apply to you! In short order you find out that they do. You may be good, but you are subject to the same kind of almost insurmountable brick walls others have run into headfirst. You sink into the quicksand and lose your focus as you flail away.

2. Alternatively, you have reached a point in your established business where you are losing customers as quickly, or quicker than you are earning new ones. The struggle means you have to trim your overheads. You cut marketing budgets first. Wrong. The quicksand engulfs you.

3. You have beaten the odds. You have a thriving enterprise and are rightfully proud of your accomplishments. However, complacency also creates a paradox.

   - Your rapid growth has made funders and even investors nervous, as rapid growth often does, and growth funds are becoming harder to acquire. You assume they will "come around." And they don't, or do so too cautiously to do you any good.

   - Your inventory includes a number of dead-end products that have outlived customers' needs and demands. They will all eventually sell, right? Well, maybe very discounted, and not quickly enough to generate cash flow.

   - Your staff has become complacent, coasting on old laurels, still delivering, but growth has slowed.

   - Competitors are stealing market share, and all-the-while your blinders approach refuses to acknowledge that markets are finite. Your base is being peeled away.

   - Technology and design have, or are in the process of leapfrogging you, and you have not prepared for this eventuality.

You are, knowingly or unknowingly, in the grips of quicksand, sinking without possibly even knowing it.

Hindsight has often proven herself to be a deflating seductress. A perfect example is the case of a past technology innovation client of mine.

This company invented a gizmo, quite clever, and one that proved to fill a market gap, at that time. Within six months, they went from start-up to revenues of over $10 million per month. The founders' inflated egos disregarded the counter-intuitive warning signs.

The banks questioned the validity of the revenue numbers and put them on a short lease which restricted their ability to meet massive market opportunities.

The owners became obsessed with rewarding themselves, using valuable cash flow to pay for luxury toys and nouveau-riche mansions.

Instead of continuing new product development, the owners convinced themselves, and them alone, that they had the final word in gizmos. They were so wrong.

Instead of dealing with the forewarning noise, the owners surrounded themselves with buffer footmen who were tasked with dealing with issues well above their pay grades. The owners could not get their now-pristine hands dirty anymore.

Despite my efforts to haul them kicking and screaming into reality, the company went into a fatal tailspin when a competitor created a faster, better, cheaper version of the gizmo that reflected new technology. Quicksand engulfed my client and left no trace, no remains, not even a pair of Lamborghini leather driving gloves emblazoned with "What Me Worry?."

Entrepreneurial success demands extreme diligence. Success is not guaranteed. It is earned by those forever aware about everything in their sandbox, and ahead of them, and open to strategic advice delivered gently, and often times less so.

Workbook

1. Have you ever found yourself in a situation where your business was in jeopardy?
   - How did you handle it?
   - What did you learn from it?
2. Do you have an exit strategy, just in case?
3. Do you consider your business invulnerable?
   - If yes, how can you bullet-proof it?
   - If no, what are the vulnerabilities you need to be steadfastly diligently track?
4. How do you best handle weak spots in your business armor? What can you do to better cope, personally, with potential quicksand?
5. How far do you think ahead?
6. How often do you act on your own advice? List a few samples and the outcomes.

What's With This Quicksand Stuff?

Eeyore, Winnie the Pooh's sad little donkey friend, is a natural tour guide for the quicksand pit so often referred to in this book.

They're funny things, Accidents. You never have them till you're having them.

From pending problems and darkish clouds on the horizon, to being "up the creek" or, worse yet, heading over the falls, the pathway to the business quicksand is littered with stuck entrepreneurs. Don't be one of them.

It's the only cloud in the sky and it's drizzling, right on me. Somehow, I'm not surprised.

Some quicksand is unavoidable. Did anyone ever imagine that a madman from Russia would turn the world and the global economy on edge? Fundamentals like energy, wheat and grain, supply chains, and other "stuff" we just take for granted?

The sky has finally fallen. Always knew it would.

Business itself is never calm, or terribly straightforward and predictable. You need the energy to challenge and change, to plot your own course, and to avoid the avoidable.

I'm not going to do nothing any more. Never again? Well, not so much.

Management by crisis, surrounded by unabated flames, is no way to run a business. You cannot and should not plan or run a business in an agitated state, or a stubborn mindset cemented in outdated thinking. The energy and willpower to recover are far greater that the effort it takes to stay attuned to your market, customers and team.

Could be worse. Not sure how, but it could be.

That represents the core of this book; the more I question and prod you, the greater the chances that you can accommodate and welcome change. You will be a happier and more fruitful businessperson, unlike Eeyore.

My eyes are open, but my mind is asleep.

This book is not intended to make light of anyone's shortcomings. I have plenty of my own flaws to deal with (you should also have met my ex-partner). So, I focus on the potentially fatal behavior, habits, and inactions that can get you in trouble. Stuck, means really stuck.

Finally, experts say that if you stay on course, there is a 78.6 percent greater chance to succeed, and a 46.5 percent chance of reaching your lofty goals. Who are these "experts" that deliver this kind of bunk? Statistics don't lie, but liars figure.

You can believe in me. Why? I have been there, having been immersed up to my "boys" in quicksand more than once. But I escaped, clawed my way out. And learned my lessons. I stay alert and reactive. If you don't fail sometimes, you will likely never succeed.

And believe in yourself and your ability to recognize the need to change. Forewarned is forearmed.

It never hurts to keep looking for sunshine.

Business storytelling and sharing experiences without preaching or taking any pretentious high ground is important. Just think of me as the somewhat offbeat but perspicacious business mentor. Like if Eeyore had a positive twin.

You're braver than you believe, stronger than you seem and smarter than you think.

Believe it.

Workbook

1. Can you define the events in your business that are leading you to, or have brought you to the quicksand pit?
2. What specific areas are you biggest weaknesses, and why?
3. What remedial action have you taken to extricate yourself?
4. How has that worked out for you? What were the results of your effort?

How Did You Even Wander Into the Quicksand?

I do not make a habit of wandering into a quicksand ambush. I avoid purposely committing an act of entrepreneurial suicide by doing or not doing something I was supposed to do, or not supposed to do. It gets confusing when we blindside ourselves. But follies happen, and there are consequences to be dealt with.

It's a rude awakening when you have one foot sinking into the sandpit and an expression of "what the hell?" adorning your brow. Five minutes ago, you were so happy, content with the world, daydreaming about what else you can conquer, and then "wham."

We get so distracted and sidetracked by "stuff," usually other shiny opportunities or painful issues, that we misstep our way directly into quicksand quagmires. You just find yourself there, sinking. Stuck. Searching for a handhold.

Congrats. You are a "Stuck Entrepreneur."

It also begs the question; how did you even wander into this turmoil? Even more important is determining how you did not see it coming, or you did see it looming, but did little to evade it?

Experience has shown these to be the main lapses that lead to perilous quicksand pitfalls.

- **Knee-jerk decision making:** Simply making decisions too hastily, or without considering all the trickle-down consequences.
- **Acting out of convenience:** When it is easier just to deal with a matter quickly, without weighing options.
- **Pushed into it:** Taking action to play "catch up" with competitors or market shifts you may not have been tracking. Expeditious, yes. Prudent, not always. Stepping into quicksand? Often.

- **Complacency:** Ego over reason. You are the best at what you do. Your business is the best in the market. You coast, until the footsteps behind you get louder and some degree of panic sets in. Panic ensues. Peril follows closely behind it.
- **Greed:** This masks any number of pathways into the quicksand. It is a core fault in the greedy businesspersons' makeup and blindspots. Greed blinds reason.
- **Cannot face the truth:** Businesses are constantly bombarded with enforced change; markets, demographics, competition, supply chains, technology, and a slew of other impacting challenges. You need to accept change. Burying your head in the sand is not a workable strategy.
- **Risk-taking:** Taking risks beyond your comfort levels, or your abilities to manage significant risk is a formula for disaster, and a one-way ticket to the depths of the quicksand field. Business does not imply Russian Roulette.

Prevention and preparation are key. Here are some key suggestions that can help you avoid the quicksand pitfalls.

1. Review every aspect of your business and work to identify existing and pending issues that demand mitigating action. Review and update this every month. Keep it current.
2. Set "Reaction Triggers," the point at which you realistically must act. "Must" is the trigger's principal call to action.
3. For every action, develop a "go/no go" process. Not every problem needs remediation. Some can simply be dropped instead of attempting circumvention. Don't ignore them, just get rid of them, period. And that includes nonperforming employees. It sounds heartless, but your survival calls for it.
4. There should be no surprises in your business life. If there are, you need to remove any blinders that shield your line of vision.
5. When faced with a pending trip to the quicksand trap, train yourself to focus on "what can I do now" and not "how come this happened?" Don't waste time pitying yourself. "Why me" is not a solution. This requires conditioning yourself on how to react to anything thrown at you.

Workbook

1. Do you identify yourself with any of the listed lapses and shortfalls expounded in this chapter? List which ones and try to explain why.
2. Develop a framework for change right here and now.
3. Are you a cyborg? Everyone has flaws. Rethink. Then have another shot at your own lapses and shortfalls.
4. Do you take any awareness/sensitivity training to keep you finely tuned to everything around you? If not, please do so. It will make you a more reactive person in your business and personal life as well. What is out there for you? Contact them now.
5. Have you surrounded yourself with like-minded people who can be your business bodyguards? If not, why not? Think about your areas of shortcoming that can be downloaded to others. What might they be?
6. Who can be a mentor/sounding board for you?

Hitting Closer to Home

If you are reading this book, you are likely stuck, or stumbling toward "stuckdom." It's a dark place, well off the beaten path of successful business. Don't you want to know why you are here? What punched your ticket? I would.

Just as important is recognizing what got you here, and why you somehow stepped right into chaos, launching the kind of turmoil that can exact a high, sometimes fatal price.

Nobody is predestined to flounder, so was it a serious error in judgment? A flawed decision-making process? A lapse, gaffe, glitch, or miscue? An unanticipated tilt in your world?

You cannot fix things until you recognize why they broke. This discourse is not for whiners and crybabies. Please leave your excuses at the door.

Do you recognize anything about yourself below? Even partially? Be honest. Let's see if we can get your mojo back on track.

1. You got into business because of a dream, a vision. Nobody forced you into it. You took the conscious decision to pursue this exciting opportunity. It was compelling. The sparkle is gone now, or fading, or overshadowed by the reality of being in business. That, in itself, can be a grinding bore. How would you recapture that entrepreneurial spark (or do you even still want to)?

2. The viability for your venture has taken a hit; competition, lagging market interest, changing tastes, and needs. You are wallowing, or anchored to the original business model and unwilling or unable to change. It's time to assess your primary business basic assumptions, adapt, or move on. Create a new, more responsive "Business Model Version 2." Drifting into the quicksand should not be an option.

3. It's tougher being in business than you had thought. Now that the rose-colored glasses are off, the nitty is pretty gritty. It's a lot of work; the risks are greater and the challenge is now more real to you. Recommit yourself to the new reality. Stand fast. Pick your battles

and new quests carefully. Understand that the work to get where you want to be just makes it more rewarding when you do finally arrive, and you likely will.

4. The work habits you have developed are not serving you well in the entrepreneurial world. Stuff is falling through the cracks. Important stuff. Big cracks. The consequences are that you may be feeling pressure to perform without the ability (or interest) to do so. Find out what is not working, what new skillsets or work priorities need to be adopted. Training may be called for. Remaining immovable is a formula for failure. Delegate, contract out, delegate (once more for emphasis) the grunt stuff that weighs you down and eats up your energy. Change or quit.

5. You may have always been a loner, or someone who has followed the direction of others. Now your role has changed. You need people around you; a team to support you; those to whom you can delegate; advisors who can provide some objectivity and direction; and importantly, a network of connections you can do business with, get referrals from, and establish your place in the business community. You don't have to do it all alone. That's just asking too much of yourself.

6. You second guess the value or merit of your products or services, and worry about meeting customer needs, when, in fact, they are likely dealing with you because of... you. You are the brand, the face of your business. More than likely what you are selling is just fine, but you may be lacking the confidence to be the company cheerleader.

7. The business responsibilities you are taking on as your own may not be the ones that need your magic touch. Maintaining a headlock on what you just like doing may not reflect what needs your attention. Focus. Prioritize. Do what's really important. Get unstuck.

8. As an entrepreneur, you likely get distracted by "the shiny coin on the road." The very next opportunity. My mother always used to lecture me "Eat your dinner before you go out to play." Good advice, Mom. Learn to focus and stay on track. Once your current business is successful and you have built a team to help run it, then, and only then can you permit yourself the luxury of searching out your next business opportunity. There will always be some shiny coins on the horizon.

We have all been through this. I have juggled several enterprises, each one becoming progressively more demanding of my time and effort. I learned my lesson by almost burning myself out. I came pretty close.

You learn that there is a difference between giving up and knowing when you have had enough. Elon Musk's mayhem at Twitter exemplifies stretching yourself too thin to perform. Isn't Tesla, SpaceX, The Boring Company, Neuralink, and the Musk Foundation considered overreach? Phew! Don't let your ego drive your potential downfall.

Personally, I had to force myself to focus on what business provided me, right now, with the results and gratification I needed. The rest I placed on the back burner and actually returned to several of them as time permitted.

The ones that had a degree of longevity were the ones waiting for my return. The fads burnt themselves out quickly, thank goodness. I never really trusted the lava lamps, and Rubik's Cube just confounded me. Glad they're gone.

There is a disorderly order to business.

Hopefully you recognize the mantras that run throughout all of the above; keep moving forward, change, and adapt. The corollary is that not doing so will trap you in the quicksand, and the longer you wait, the deeper and faster you will sink.

Workbook

Before you can absorb all the worthwhile advice in this book, you need to understand why you got here, and exactly where "here" is.

1. How did you get here? What brought you here? Events or circumstance within your control, or not?
2. If they were within your control, why didn't you react, or, if you did, what was the outcome? Is the situation fixable? If so, then how?
3. Did you build any strategies to deal with any future downsides?

This is an important task. Do it thoroughly, introspectively and honestly. It will be worth it.

Trust me. Been there, done that, and better for it.

Dump That Nonperforming Albatross

The businessperson who collects or hoards especially unneeded items is mired in the malaise of "stuck-hood." The costs and impact of this coveting are staggering, often disorienting to your team and customers, and sometimes even fatal.

This includes any number of packrat uncalled-for caches of goodies. Do you recognize anything about these tendencies to stockpile?

- Nonperforming staff, whose work causes yet more work for others around them, and for you too.
- Ineffective managers and executive decision makers who have risen well above their level of competence, and are incurring unnecessary costs and putting your business at risk.
- Severely stifled employees, generally friends and relatives, cast into positions of authority without the skillsets to do little other than be parasites in the business hierarchy.
  - *That brother-in-law or nephew who needed a job? Who is taking on extra responsibilities to cover their ineptitude? Perhaps you are allergic to confrontation. That is also quite common amongst stuck businesspeople. Be bold. Decisive. Unafraid. Your well-being is the only critical consideration.*
  - *It is not a sign of disloyalty to monitor nonperformer team members and dump them, or adapt products or services to make them more market-friendly. That is called "survival."*
- Products that have slow turnover rates and require huge discounts just to move them. Eventually, that inventory will be written off to the disadvantage of your bottom line. Take the hit now.
- Services that are outdated, obsolete, or have been leapfrogged by competition, technology, or the ever-changing marketplace have no place in your business.

- For multiple-location businesses, you tend to keep them all, even where some do not work for your company anymore. You coddle all the people there. You know them and their families. Instead of consolidating locations and transferring or reducing staff, you sigh and keep writing those rent and overhead checks. You are smitten with stuck.
- Opportunities are exciting, but some do not work. They become a burden, beyond capable of being resuscitated by CPR. But you are loath to dump them even after a lengthy trial period, because just maybe they will come to life. Having deadwood projects on your plate is just more for you to worry about. Sell, backburner, or dump nonperforming opportunities.
- Your suppliers are the same suppliers that your parents or grandparents worked with in the business, except they are not the same. Prices are out of line, quality is less so, and service is unreliable. Your supply chain is in danger. Think change. Old allegiances can only take you so far. The market is crowded with suppliers committed to best service your needs. Find them. Set up new sourcing avenues and supply chains. Get unstuck.

Why then does the stuck entrepreneur circle the quicksand pit? It would seem to those rationally minded that it is common sense to dump what (and who) does not work. Then why do we hang on?

- Fear of change is a major factor. People naturally abhor change, but those who are stuck often find change painful. This includes the stuck person's irrational fear of "intolerable backlash" that they fear change can provoke. It's easier to just ignore the need to change and learn to live with the consequences. Even so, a quick fallout is better than living with a lingering pain.
- We are all reasonably sensible and rational humans (with the exceptional of one of my past partners, but that's a story for another time). The idea of dumping anything that is nonperforming is often deemed as a personal failure by the stuck entrepreneur. Their sensibilities are offended. This

heightened sensitivity needs to be capped. In business, reason needs to prevail over emotion.

- History creates a scenario which, to most of us, is the basis and foundation for change. For the stuck, history is often immovable, even when everything around them is relentlessly shifting.
- The stuck businessperson develops an unusual tolerance; comfort with the uncomfortable. This status quo is something they need to, but often do not challenge.

"Don't be afraid to dump the non-performing" is not advice. It is more of a forewarning. Here are a few strategies that can actually help the stuck businessperson face and deal with the consequences of unacceptable performance. Dealing with people does not have to be messy.

1. Set a division of responsibility as well as performance targets for your people.
2. Carry out regular staff performance reviews. Reward those who have delivered, and issue warnings to those who fall short. With the latter, use the "three strikes and you're out" rule, and let everyone know it.
3. If you sell products, create management reports that measure annual stock turnovers as well as product returns and customer complaints. These quantifiable factors can provide even the stuck businessperson with the impetus to act. Product returns can also indicate that you may need to change suppliers or fix any in-house production head-aches, so pay attention to rejects flowing in from customers.
4. If you sell services, create reports that measure the trend of revenues generated by each service. This is especially effective if the service is "stand-alone" as opposed to part of a package. Use the results to make any "keep/dump" decisions.
5. Gross margins are good indicators as to whether your products or services are contributing to your financial health. "Marginal" is not a category you need to live with, unless it's for a lost leader. Keep job costs that give you the kind of feedback you need for deci-sion making. Keep the profitable stuff. Dump the rest. Don't let deadheads linger.

6. Once you make any staffing decisions, especially those pertaining to employees or even that brain-damaged nephew who messes up regularly, it is easier for the stuck to delegate any action (such as reprimanding or firing) to an intermediary.

7. There is no need to adopt an extreme strategy, like the car dealership manager who fires the lowest performing salesman at the end of each month. That's kind of inhuman.

Dumping the nonperforming albatross demands a diminished emotional attachment to the 'dumpee', in conjunction with your willingness and ability to act. Make a decision, take action, and make it easier on your mental well-being, and your balance sheet.

Workbook

1. Think about any weak links in your business; people, sales force, products/services, branding and market positioning, or anything else you are aware of.

   (a) How long have you known about each one you identified in this exercise?

   (b) What are the extra costs or lost revenues related to each?

   (c) What corrective action have you taken? How did that work for you?

   (d) Can you still take effective corrective action? If so, what?

   (e) What action was recommended to you by others you trust?

      (i) Did you act? What was the outcome?

      (ii) You didn't! Why not?

Does This Make Me Look Fat?

The other day I couldn't help myself eavesdropping on a 60ish-year-old guy with a coiffed gray mane, wearing jean overalls with one strap stylishly drooping off his shoulder, and sporting unlaced skater sneakers. He was buying Viagra at the pharmacy.

Actually, it wasn't tough listening in since he proudly bellowed his Viagra order to the pharmacist and then looked around, smirking, as he surveyed the room for a hopefully adoring and jealous audience.

He then kind of dance-stepped out, squeezed himself into his bright red Mini Cooper and zoomed away noisily. It was a laughably bizarre moment.

What have we become? A nation obsessed, eager to upsell ourselves? A need to create an image of ourselves as how we want others see us? The answer is sadly but resolutely "yes."

It's no different in business.

We package ourselves. We dress the part, shopping at the boutiques (not stores, OMG) that cater to people like us. Of course, we need that $250 silk tie and $3,500 suit or those $750 designer pumps!

We primp and preen to appeal to strangers, friends, and try to show up business foes and out-glitz competitors. We drive the status car. We eat where we can be recognized, even obsequiously acknowledged by the maître d'. Our networking small talk consists of the hottest vacation spots, the biggest "scores," and the most outrageous lies.

And while it all may sound glamorous, it is a dangerous behavior. The alarm bells should be peeling as you dig yourself into a possibly fictional or overextended character role that you now have to maintain and continually embellish. It is not an easy task.

Punishment for any transgressions is you being ostracized by your peers, and that translates to lost business and missing out on opportunities.

So, look out for the quicksand pit of botox'd happiness. Just tone it down.

And if you see an older guy cruising in his red Mini Cooper, thumping on the steering wheel and humming tunes you barely recognize, smile and appreciate that he is reveling in his own little world where he is deliriously happy and everybody knows and loves him.

Workbook

1. List five things you do to package yourself that is outside your norm/comfort zone.
2. List five reasons why you feel the need to do so.

Leaving Academia and Bumping Into the Real World

For years, you have likely enjoyed the womb-like safety of academia where the impact of any mistakes or shortfalls on your part reflect, worst case, in a lower score on an assignment or course credit. Boo hoo. The potential repercussion of messing up in college is like a Band-Aid on a skinned knee compared to the injurious fallout that real-world business can exact on you.

Get prepared. That means undertaking a balancing act. How? While still in university, dip a toe into the business world. Get acquainted with what you may well be in for when you leave your safety net.

Enjoy the "wins" and lick your wounds. You will likely experience both.

1. Without forsaking your academic pursuits, plan a business venture and launch it, generally without strangling and risking your equity, time, and resources. Think of something you have some experience in, or monetizing a hobby, skill or interest. Run it. Carve out a market niche. Take some calculated risks. Make some nonlethal mistakes. Earn customers. Get yelled at by customers and learn to cope. Make a profit, or lose a little (but not much). In short, be an entrepreneur while you are still learning textbook business and entrepreneurship.

   One key lesson you will learn is that textbook learning is often sugar-coated, while real-world learning toughens you up. You will also learn where the quicksand traps are hiding out, and how to deftly side-step them. This is kind of being the prestuck entrepreneur and dealing effectively with it.

2. Unless you are a trust fund baby, you will have to work while in college. Option number two finds you toiling for dollars, and while it is attractive to seek companionship tending bar at Enritzio's (or "My Laughing Death") Lounge, instead, find an apprenticeship or

part-time gig at a business that reflects your entrepreneurial interests. Learn everything about them; how they market themselves, how they operate, how they treat customers, how they stack up against direct competitors, how they treat their people, and, well, anything that impacts upon their business.

While I attended university, majoring in psychology with a goal of going into this field, I landed a job at a large psychiatric hospital called The Protestant Hospital for the Insane. It was obviously not a time of social sensitivity.

I experienced and "lived" the horrors of it all in terms of patient treatment, lack of any meaningful therapy and medieval living conditions. Pharmacology ruled. Healing was governed by dumb luck, not by care. Staff training consisted of a one-page handout, mostly extolling to "be careful." Shock therapy was still a forerunner to compassion. In short, opposite to everything I was simultaneously learning in university.

Rather than preparing me for the real world, I realized that I could not make any meaningful contribution to what I had witnessed and decided to move into another field.

In hindsight, that proved to be an incredibly valuable lesson for me; experiencing real-world while still under the spell of academia.

Your experience in this alternate employment universe may well impact your career or entrepreneurial journey. If that happens, it's a good thing. You will thank me for suggesting that you rethink, refocus, and maybe sprint away in another direction.

Workbook

1. Identify the top ten companies or organizations that reflect your business interests and could likely be role models for you.
2. Apply for some part-time position. Work for free (or almost) if you need to.
3. Make a list of questions you might have. This should become an ongoing, always updated list, including any differences you uncover between academia and your employer.
4. Speak to people. Make friends, some of whom may even be useful after you graduate.
5. Keep a journal of what you learn.

Afraid of Success

"I've had many problems in my life, and most of them have never happened." Until I was able to grasp that simple doctrine, I was a stuck entrepreneur; paralyzed by shadows, possibly like you might be, or might well become.

And then, there was an "Aha Moment," where reasoning started edging out the murkiness of my apprehensions. The clarity of the moment was blinding.

It may seem awkward to reflect on the oxymoron "coping with success" and offering strategies herein to recognize yourself as being "successful." That speaks to the pressures, real or perceived, that we put onto ourselves, or are thrust upon us by others.

This chapter is dedicated to identifying and overcoming the often-ethereal fear of success.

1. It is appropriate to set your targets high, slightly higher than your reach. But many of us see ourselves as the next Steve Jobs, when, in fact, we would be satisfied with far less. If you are forever chasing an elusive dream of unrealistic expectations, you will likely be constantly unhappy, fearful, and see yourself as a failure.

2. Self-confidence and belief in oneself are tall stepping stones. If you misstep and fail, you will learn and be stronger. If you dwell on failure, you will fail, possibly over and over again, with each setback slowly bankrupting your entrepreneurial courage.

3. Does asking for outside advice, help, counsel, or mentoring make you feel inadequate? Fear of being perceived as weak? Nobody knows everything, and that includes you. Even the best businesspeople seek out others. Just look at any Board of Directors of some of the highest profile companies, and recognize the wealth of knowledge that successful businesspeople assemble.

4. There is a well-entrenched bogeyperson that haunts those afraid of success; fear of rejection. Understand that you will be rejected, and possibly often. With each "no" find out why, and better your

approach for next time. At some point, the "yes"s' will make the "no"s' a trivial annoyance, but you have to get there.

5. Business is not personal. It is a vehicle to express your entrepreneurial vision. It may feel part of you, your "baby," but when businesses fail, or skip a heartbeat or two, it's not you that is being rejected. It's the business. Toughen up. If someone like Steve Jobs spent all his time sulking every time he was beaten up, where would we be today?

6. Success is often hindered by the mental exercise of you worrying about what others think about you or your business. Understand that, in today's hectic business world, most of us have enough trouble concentrating on our own businesses without the luxury of thinking about yours. The digital world has outpaced our ability to focus. With the average visitor to your website or social media page staying logged in for eight seconds or less, you can rest assured that any wayward thoughts about you and your business will be fleeting at best. You are safe.

7. Assume you may never be 100 percent ready. Examine what frightens you, and whether it is rational (money, skills, etc.) or irrational (just about everything else). If it's rational, develop a game plan to deal with it. If it's irrational, just assume that experience and failure will be wise taskmasters. Nobody is ever 100 percent ready. Lower your expectations to "ready-enough."

8. Worried about not being able to maintain your business? Most businesses do not exhibit meteoric rises. They chug along, growing steadily, or just sustain themselves at a certain level. Learn to be satisfied with what you have built.

9. You will likely never be over all your fears, and to a certain extent, your apprehensions are your safety net. Learn to listen to that nagging little voice, but you also need to learn to tell it when to "shut up." Are you perfect? No. You never will be. Accept that you are likely good enough to be a player. So, play.

There are limitless reasons that you can use to justify your fear of success; anxiety, bad past experiences, poor self-image, self-loathing, and so on. However, these are not reasons. They are excuses. Deal with them and tuck them away out of sight and mind, and get on with it. Or find a safe, boring job.

Workbook

If you have fought your way through this chapter, then "fear of success" is a demon you may be facing.

1. List five of the most debilitating aspects of business that are impacting your ability to succeed or, feeding your fear of success.
2. For each one, try to identify the rational or irrational source of that fear. List them.
3. For each of the above, determine if they are inflexible or changeable.
   - If they are intractable, can you live with them without any undue fear? If so, what behavior modifications do you need to adopt?
   - If they can be changed, how do you propose to do it?

Using People and Being Used. It's Not as Bad as It Sounds.

Using people in business is wrong. It's evil. Narcissistic. Immoral. Using people as stepping stones is, well, just abhorrent. If that is your intransigent thinking, then you are stuck, and here's why.

Business relationship-building is not a group therapy session. It is a collection of users who learn and practice the skills of using.

Let's start by defining "using others" in business. It is building relationships for the sole purpose of creating opportunities for you, seeking favors, searching for leads, contacts and connections, and even pursuing advice and counsel. **There are two important corollaries here.**

1. To use others, you need to open yourself up to being used….and you will be.
2. When you allow yourself to be used, you are accumulating favors. Those "get out of jail cards" (perhaps not a great analogy, but I think you understand) can prove to be invaluable when you need the issuer to reciprocate.

My contacts and network of connections have always been one of my most prized business assets. I have always nurtured and safeguarded them shamelessly, and without exception, even included the people I disliked, but knew could deliver results for me.

As self-serving as this might sound, it is a fact. Businesspeople within your circle or sphere of interest beget introductions to yet more connections who beget memberships into other close-knit groups which beget business opportunities. And so, the begetting continues to roll.

I have met and even mentored numerous entrepreneurs who shuddered at the concept of using people. Perhaps the terminology is the turnoff. Let's try cross-pollination, mutual exchange, asking, befriending, seeking out, or, my favorite, accommodation of favors. Does that make it easier?

As a general rule in my own networking circles, I playact the role of an interested and involved participant. I ask pointed questions and gush (ugh) at others' success stories. I never question anything that I hear that I know is embellished. It is not my place to admonish any braggadocio, that is, blowhard. Rather, I am receptive and remain visibly (but distantly) intrigued. But there is a purpose to all of this.

I see each player as a "multiplier," someone who could open doors for me. These people are merely stepping stones who pave my pathway to other rewards. Do I like them? That never entered into it. Still doesn't. This is simply all part of well-orchestrated theatrics.

I myself never discard or avoid making and sustaining connections. Many prove to be fruitful or useful at some later date. If this sounds a bit like a scene out of *The Godfather*, it kind of is. ("One day I may call upon you...")

There is a natural order to things. In any viable business relationship, you likely get stepped on as often as you step on others.

- You seek out funding and investor contacts.
- You pursue business leads.
- You piggyback with others to reach new markets and opportunities outside your current grasp.
- You seek out introductions to those who can help you achieve objectives such as advice on issues, input on new products or services you are considering, and much more.

The stuck businessperson needs to accept this "use-be used" doctrine and enhance their game plan.

The key here is to be a proactive player.

1. Identify what you need, what gaps you need to fill, who you want to deal with.
2. List out the people you know who can deliver the goods, or act as "multipliers," for example, facilitators who can open doors for you.

3. Work to understand what you have that you can offer in return, even a future I.O.U. favor.

4. Facilitate the user-to-user conversation.

5. Ignoring or marginalizing relationship-building is a certain trip to the quicksand.

6. Do not write-off any contacts. Everyone serves a purpose, now or downstream.

7. Damaged relationships are often not recoverable, or, at best, can be re-established but at a far lower, less-trusting, less-giving level.

8. Continually build your network. Some participants will drop out. Stay in touch with them. New players will buy a ticket in. Become their friend and supportive ally.

9. Give leads and opportunities as much as you get. Don't be just a "taker." People get wise to takers and shut them out.

10. Become the chameleon in the group, and give only as much background and personal information as you need to in order to punch your membership card.

There are, of course, exceptions, and that is the one-way user who takes, or demands, but gives back little. They are easily identified; selfish, egocentric, live on favors, have little regard for inconveniencing you, are selectively and gushingly nice as part of their act to get what they want from you, and will betray your trust in a heartbeat. They are obvious, and almost entertaining to watch.

A number of years ago I was on a speakers' circuit and that including networking at each event. There was one individual who seemed to attend almost every workshop, and like clockwork, he would approach me and foist his business card on me, and almost frisk me for leads. He offered nothing in return. He was a taker.

Once I realized this, I started collecting his business cards and carried them with me to the speaking engagements. On one occasion, when I had enough of him, I waited for him to hit on me again, which he predictably did. As he reached into his pocket to drag out yet another card, I said "I don't think I ever gave you my business card" and proceeded to offer him a handful of his cards back to him. He never approached me again.

A necessary word about abhorrent contacts you encounter along the way. Yes, they can be deplorable alpha males or females crying out for attention. Yes, they can challenge you to a "pissing contest," which you will willingly lose. Yes, they are innervating. But they are the easiest to prey upon. They are vulnerable and generally ego-driven. Providing you access to leads, introductions, and other opportunities feeds their fragile egos. Use them. Exploit the referrals. Play the game.

The bottom line is that using people is fair game, as long as you abide by the two-way-street principal and avoid the blatant takers. For the hesitant stuck entrepreneur, call it by any other name, but, by all means, step up to the plate.

Workbook

1. Are there businesspeople you want to meet? List five.
2. What can these people do for you?
3. What could you give back to them in return?
4. How would you propose to get to them? Directly? Through a multiplier like a business acquaintance, or lawyer, or accountant?
5. Are there business associations or series of events or conferences that offer greater access to the kinds of people you can use? List five that you can think of and prioritize them in terms of costs and availability of your time.

Be Selfish. Be Unapologetically Selfish.

The stuck entrepreneur who is characteristically easy going, altruistic, and noble in attitude and action had better learnt quickly that this is a tough, selfish world, and business exacerbates that mean streak.

If I have described you, then you had better pay attention to how the real business world eats its young, and what you can do to better understand your environ, and learn to cope.

If you identify yourself as an entrepreneur, you should be unapologetic about being selfish. Others may not understand, or appreciate your vision, but you aren't building their future and working toward their happiness. You should be selfish in pursuing your own passion. Your game. Your rules. Your truth.

Richard Dawkins wrote about "the Selfish Gene" as it referred to DNA, and its sole purpose to survive. That, however, has now been kidnapped into understanding human behavior. We are all selfish creatures, some more so than others, and some more blatantly committed to self-preservation. In business, that's called entrepreneurship, and being selfish is a very good ideal.

In business, selfishness translates to passion, drive, and determination. It's okay to act without feeling guilty. The pursuits of achieving freedom and control are not negative. It's who we are, as entrepreneurs.

"What's in it for me" ('WIIFM') is a marketing golden rule. Whatever you produce or sell needs to meet the identified needs of the marketplace and the end user. Your opinion counts for very little since it is the customer/buyer who reaches for his or her credit card, not you.

The dedicated entrepreneur has adopted WIIFM into their own personal motives, namely, the raison d'etre behind being in business. And we have accepted that being selfish is good for you, without any negative connotations or fallout. Have we talked ourselves into accepting this behavior? Possibly, to a certain extent, but it's not all bad.

- We often prioritize our business above almost everything. Our drive to succeed is primal. That is a positive selfish trait.
- We strive to lead and control. That allows entrepreneurs to become unabashed innovators and market disrupters. Again, selfishness is viewed as affirming.
- Selfishness gives you space to focus on new opportunities, proactively dealing with challenges, and even emotional respites to devote to friends and family, or outside interests. Even entrepreneurs deserve to be happy.
- Being selfish makes you are "provider," a role model for others, and someone who strives to fulfill their own game plan for business, and for life. And while you may not care as much about others, they will care about you.

There is always a flipside to almost everything. Selfishness can morph dangerously into you becoming the black sheep by adopting the selfish gene and employing deceptive and questionable ethics as part of your business behavior arsenal.

The calculus of criminals is best understood as a set of rational trade-offs between the benefits of crime and the cost of punishment, discounted by the probability of detection.

—Garry Becker, 1968.

This rational has a certain twisted logic to it that falls within the purview of the entrepreneur who stretches the flexibility or elasticity of behavior and ethics to the breaking point, and possibly beyond; winning at any cost and with little concern for others, or any impactful damage to others.

And that is where selfishness becomes bad. Don't go there. There are boundaries.

Being selfish does not give you a pass to being a narcissistic pirate. On the contrary. Selfishness can be a valuable tool for growing your business based on exceptional focus and leadership while steadfastly steering your way through the ever-changing course of entrepreneurship.

Workbook

1. Having absorbed all of the aforementioned, create a chart to identify your personal and business selfish behavior. The left column is your personal life; the right column is your business world. Are you comfortable with these? Anything worth toning down, or building on?

2. Anger is often a selfish kneejerk reaction. Name five occasions where you have made decisions based on anger? How did these work out for you?

Don't Be a Sorrowful Entrepreneur

Do you blame others for your failures? It's never you. In fact, it is anyone within berating distance; business associates, partners, friends, family, contractors, and the family dog. Or could it be that the planets are not aligned, Venus is not lined up with Mars? Or perhaps your horoscope has predicted tough times ahead. It's all "pity-me" thinking. The only things lining up are you and failure. Time to step away from the quicksand.

In all seriousness, there are a number of critical features that nudge (or thrust) you toward the quicksand, and once stuck, it is difficult to extract yourself. Learn about the hazard warnings, the mindset of failure, and the behavior that hurries you along toward the pit.

1. You have developed a product or service in an ivory tower, with little or no consideration to what the market needs. You just assumed it would be snapped up. You possibly even did some focus groups, but of course your friends said "great" and your mom said she was so proud of you. Seriously? Hope you enjoyed the ego trip. This closed-mindedness can be lethal.
2. You have a market-ready product or service that does lots but doesn't really do anything particularly well. App and software developers are often accused of this. The result is market adoption that is hesitant at best. Simple advice? Ask first, build later.
3. Here's one relating to both of the above.
   Customers want to know what value you will provide. Have a value proposition (i.e., a statement that summarizes why a customer would choose your product or service and the benefits of dealing with you) that resonates with a customer pain point.
   —Kyle Wong, Pixlee CEO
4. You think no one can do it as well as you can, so you do it all, including stuff you only have a marginal knowledge about, and spend time learning about instead of doing what you do best.

Learn to delegate and be fearless downloading your unwanted tasks or unfamiliar/uncomfortable areas of responsibilities. It's okay to say "I don't know this." It doesn't make you a failure. It identifies you as someone who lives by their strengths and recognizes their weaknesses.

5. You are big on prioritizing, but you rank those priorities based on how easy they are, and not necessarily by the order of their importance and their ability to positively impact your business. That's just the laziness of convenience.

6. Risk is part of business. It's difficult for you, since you do not tolerate setbacks well. Risk is a stepping stone to success. Accept risk, or go flip burgers.

7. You are a perfectionist, an overbuilder. You feel your business model needs to be 100 percent, not 99 percent. You overthink. Meanwhile your competitors are leapfrogging you like mad. Have the confidence to launch what the market is seeking and that is rarely 100 percent perfection.

8. Instead of learning from your mistakes, you pout. You get depressed and discouraged. It's what is referred to as the "trough of sorrow" where dejected entrepreneurs reside, often indefinitely, unable or unwilling to claw out and try again, try better.
   Struggle is where greatness comes from.
                              —Ben Horowitz, investor, business author

9. You are a business startup junkie, which is fine, but stick with what is working. Don't seek out the next shiny coin on the road at the expense of your current successful business.

10. Eventually, you will lose your best people, and your focus. Bored? Sell your business and move on to something that excites you more. Stop juggling, because that one ball too many will be costly when it (or all) drops from your grasp.

I have had a number of clients, primarily in tech or biomed, that have spent tons of money, usually investors' money, to develop a widget, program, or product that was exceptional in its concept but unexceptional in its ill-thought-out marketplace. In some cases, there were no identified end users.

In one particular case, after two million dollars was spent in research and development, my first question to them after my sitting through a particularly stunning 50,000-foot graphic presentation was "who will buy this?" The CEO proudly announced that they would "simply" (and he did casually use that word far too naively) educate the market, like Apple and Starbucks did. I left the meeting with my investors in tow. Naivety has little place in business success.

Educating the market is time-consuming and costly. It is a process. There is a classic case of a coffee chain not known outside of North America who decided to introduce coffee to China. This was pre-Starbucks arriving there. Instead of waiting and riding on Starbuck's coattails, they decided to open several coffee roasters and shops throughout Beijing and Shanghai. They spent millions and stood by the (failed) arrogant marketing cliché "If we build it, they will come." You can figure out the rest of this sad saga.

But there is hope. All is not lost. The lesson here is to recognize the malaise of the sorrowful entrepreneur so that you will not get stuck in their business fantasies or melancholy, but instead, enjoy your entrepreneurial adventure and realize your business dream.

Workbook

1. What is your core expertise? List the top five features that make you personally outstanding. Are they working for you? Do they need revisiting?
2. Are you doing anything beyond those areas? What? Do you need to? Can you delegate?
3. Are you doing anything that is not generating money for your business? You shouldn't be.
4. What makes your product or service unique? Name five. Do they win you market recognition? Why or why not? Can you do anything better?

Mama Told You That There Would Be Days Like These

Everybody eventually puts a wheel in the ditch on the road to success, so don't think that you are special. You're not. Everybody gets here at some point. It's part of the entrepreneurial deal that you bought into.

Getting stuck is very common. Ok you're stuck, I get it, but what you really need to do now is to take a deep breath and figure out what's next.

We all like to think positively. It's the nature of the business types, so it's natural to duck or delay the obvious truth when your venture stalls. Let me guess; you're working more than ever; can't remember when you last got a new account; and you just used your personal credit card to pay this month rent. Yeah, you're stuck.

Here are some of the "stuck" milestones. How many do you recognize?

- Are you experiencing an unanticipated change in the market?
- Are you stretched and taking on too much at one time?
- Are sales falling?
- Company burn out? Everyone who was gung-ho now leaving work early?
- Are you sure that you have the right people in the right spots?
- Is the company running low on money?

I was once stuck in a classic failure that grew into a big success. Our product was in the wrong place with the wrong price and we missed our target market. In spite of all that, we knew that we had a great core idea for our business.

We kept banging our collective heads against the same wall and as things got worse, we misfired even harder. Finally, we took a step back.

We had believed that we had a great idea that our market would want, but whatever we were doing didn't work for them or us, and we had just wasted a small fortune, especially with cash flow being so tight. This nightmare inspired our big rethink.

This cathartic experience encouraged us to develop a strategy to look at other avenues that we had not yet explored. We had become blind to anything other than our original vision. That is, until we took a step into the quicksand. Sure enough, one of the alternative distribution channels that we never considered turned out to be our savior gold mine.

It's not unusual for business ventures to plateau, get stuck, or end up in the deep end and treading water. It happens to all of us. Anyone who is regarded as a success in business experiences the perils and night sweats of the "stuck" experience. Everybody!

So, the reality is that the majority of early stage companies get stuck at some point, but real entrepreneurs steady on. You wouldn't have put the effort into your business if you didn't believe that it would prosper.

When things look bleak for your business, it's time to step back and refocus on your original idea; the fundamental corner stone of your venture, not the execution that may have stalled. It's time to re-evaluate how your great initial business model went off the rails. Use the reality of this tough situation to rethink how you can better shape the future.

I know this all sounds pretty preachy, but if I could reach out and gently smack you on the side of the head, I would. The answer is within your reach. Don't let it slide by. And don't be that entombed entrepreneur that lets their vision end up in a shallow grave, or sinking away into the quicksand.

Workbook

1. State your core business value in less than 20 words.
2. Why is your original business concept so good (or is it)?
   - Is it still good? Why do you think so?
3. Why are you stuck? Do a real heart-felt analysis of what is holding you back.
4. What is the internal baggage or the external baggage that is causing your misery?

5. What priorities do you want/need to deal with to untangle the mess you are in? Slow down, step back, and you will get a clearer picture of where you are and where you are going.

6. Simplify: Go back to the original business concept. Analyze it, tweak it, and filter it to fit your new focus. How would you simplify your business? List five major changes you would consider.

What If the Worst Happened? "So What" Planning

I've had a lot of worries in my life, most of which never happened.
—Mark Twain

According to NBC News ("Better" by Today), about 85 percent of what we worry about never materializes. But worry prompts us to take action, sometimes the wrong action at the worst time, very possibly putting ourselves and our business at risk.

Worry over real or perceived challenges pushes us, sometimes even drags us toward the quicksand where decision making becomes moot. You just sink.

There was a point in my business-building career where I worried about everything. And if, miraculously, I had few hiccoughs to worry about, I created some more. Or, worse yet, I worried about worrying, or not worrying. It's a vicious, debilitating cycle that feeds on itself. However, worrying may NOT be something to worry about (pun intended) if you buy into the following "so what" planning.

Real or Not: It is critical to determine if all your hand-wringing is justified. Is the problem real? Often you need to get a second (or third) opinion from an uninvolved source you trust. Ask three people and follow the advice offered up by the majority. There will usually be some consensus among them. Some commonality of feedback.

Change: Nothing is static. The corollary is to expect change because it is inevitable. "So what" planning demands that you remain diligent to pending change in everything, from controllable impacts such as shifting markets to those beyond your control, life, world politics, and (ugh) elections. Plan for change. Lay out your options and have them at-the-ready to implement.

Several "Kicks at the Can": Entrepreneurs will generally go through several renditions of their "best business ever" over the course of their business life span. Just know that the idea of business permanence is often a fallacy. You will move on.

Learn from Failure: Often cited but difficult to swallow. The best way to accept this strategy is to research those who are now successful and look back at the setbacks they encountered. (We humans like to witness other peoples' miseries. I guess it makes ours seem less tragic.) All setbacks, in hindsight, are transparent. There is almost always a shimmering opaque haze exit at the end of that passageway.

You are Your Business: Whatever venture you launch, you are what people recognize and learn to rely on, or hopefully admire. You are the brand. Ergo, the strategy is to continually package and market yourself so that, in the event you need to switch direction in your business life, you have a robust head start. Namely, you.

Loss of a Major Client: Because you strive to diversify your client portfolio and reduce any reliance on one or two key clients, this should never happen, right? Diversify at all cost. Spread the risk instead of losing sleep.

I had the pleasure of working for a large manufacturer of musical instruments. Despite being somewhat tone-deaf and incapable of learning to play anything more complicated than a tambourine, I very much enjoyed the environment I found myself in. What I didn't like was the Sales Manager's strategy.

In order to meet his numbers quota, he negotiated discounted deals with only one department store chain whom, I knew, were not in the strongest financial health. It got to the point that 85 percent of our revenues were soon derived from this one chain who were also renowned for late payments. That terrible cash flow didn't help us one bit.

At all management meetings, I fought this uni-customer trend, predicting major difficulties for us if this chain faltered or failed. My warnings were finally heeded, but too late. The chain went bankrupt, and our company, unable to change course quickly enough, followed shortly thereafter. It did not end on a good note.

Thrill the Money People: Whoever signs the checks, invests, supplies working capital, and feeds your cash flow needs to be kept happy. Do it, and there will be less downtime worrying. The best strategy is twofold; deliver results and suck up to the moneylenders as required.

Avoid the Knee-Jerk Reaction: "So what" planning does not imply grasping at the first lifeline. Planning and preparation are important. You need options. Act, don't react.

Business is Just Business: Far too often we forget that business is not our life. It might be our lifeblood, but shouldn't be all we equate with life. That is best reserved for family, friends, and interests that make us grow and experience, well…life. Acting on "so what" contingency planning is significantly more tolerable and acceptable when we realize there's more out there.

Workbook

1. Assuming you are human and have had several crises in your business career, what were they? How (or did you) fall into them? How did you react to them? What were the outcomes?

2. For your current business, what are the top worst five things that could happen? On a scale of 1 (low) to 5 (high), what are the chances that they will actually ever materialize? And, what are the triggers that would launch them? The assumption here is that acknowledging the worst, and the initiates of the circumstances, is the core of "so what" planning.

3. If you have witnessed a business friend or associate (or competitor) goes through the crisis/worst day of their life process, what lessons can you take away from the experience?

Maybe You Just Went Into the Wrong Business?

If you can be unpleasantly surprised about something (or anything) in your business, then maybe you just went into wrong business. Think about that.

We're not talking about your choice of office furniture or dress codes. The inference here is that the surprise needs to be business-perilous, a revelation that can have dire consequences and delivers bewilderment and shock to your normally composed and manicured self.

Reality sets in. A situation or event that demands an unplanned-for response from you. Something that draws your attention away from your present course to deal with a curveball that you did not expect, or chose to ignore. Wham!

One of the doctrines of business is to be prepared. "Prepared for what?" "Why, for any old thing," replied Scouting founder Robert Baden-Powell. Coolness, composure, and forethought.

Most disasters are avoidable. Maintaining a keen sense of your business-playing field is keynote, as is predicting, and planning contingencies to deal with whatever tries to invade your space.

A judicious practice is carrying out a SWOT analysis each six months; strengths, weaknesses, opportunities, and threats. The results tell you what your company does best, and worst, what opportunities are on the horizon, and what events you normally have no control over can threaten your venture. I always made a point of being retrospective and completing a SWOT every six months. I also carried out a Personal SWOT, measuring my own performance at the helm of my company. It was very revealing, and sometimes provided a rude awakening when the indication was that my interests were slipping.

I love this next case study. It still makes me shake my head in disbelief.

I had a client who had these most glorious plans to build a luxury resort on the hurricane/tsunami/thunderstorm coast of Costa Rica.

By the time I got involved with him, he had already invested several million dollars, with the work supervised by the local contractor. My client felt it wasn't necessary for him to be on site. Misguided, arrogant, and lazy planning and thinking.

I even quoted him one of my favorite movie lines where Aladdin was sailing off on a dangerous voyage. His grandfather took him aside and said "Trust in Allah, but tie up your camel." It was such appropriate advice for my far-too-trusting client.

I warned him often about these glaring quicksand pits, but he remained oblivious to these colossal miscues. This combination of blunders was his undoing.

His unsupervised onsite manager developed a thriving side hustle business selling building materials and renting out the owners' construction equipment.

My client's business was interrupted only after the entire resort was washed away by a hurricane several weeks before the resorts' grand opening. Bottles of champagne kept getting washed back ashore for weeks afterwards, littering his beach alongside his broken hot tubs, changing cabanas and roofing.

The bereaved and disillusioned owner clung to his mantra "I didn't know. Nobody told me." Wrong. I told you. Others told you. You just didn't listen. Listening is a very important entrepreneurial skill to develop.

In another case, I was mandated to review the operation of a regional private aquarium and ocean attraction facility. It was in ugly disrepair, and the regional district was concerned about the health and safety of visitors, and staff.

Meetings with the owner were more like jousting matches. He was adamant that he did not want to invest any more money into this venture despite the fact that the attraction could be developed into a profitable regional tourist attraction. He did not see any of the issues that were glaring to outsiders, and myself.

My recommendations were quite simple. There were three options: (1) expropriate the property; (2) find a new owner; or (3) think sashimi for the aquariums' residents and tear the facility down. The sashimi option got me fired.

As an owner, it is your responsibility to be the catalyst for change. It's really a simple case of peeking beyond any blinders that may be hiding what is going on beside you, behind you, and in front of you.

As well, delegation is often spoken about in glowing terms. But it has been my experience that downloading important responsibilities encourages you to wash your hands of stuff you should really be part of. In my career, I have been accused of being a micromanager, usually muttered in disdain. However, I am proud to stay involved in almost everything around me. I vary my degree of hands-on depending on whose hands I left the responsibility with.

Delegation does not mean absolving yourself of obligations and outcomes. You should really know what's going on with every facet of your business.

And if you are uncomfortable with any of these concepts, then perhaps you went into the wrong business.

Workbook

1. Is your business your first choice for an endeavor, or was this an opportunity presented to you? How does that impact your performance?
2. Do you love your business? Justify it, or not.
3. Do you feel it is right for you, your character, your personality, and your interests?
4. Has your business given you the entrepreneurial experience (and exhilaration) you were seeking?
5. Do you feel there are elements of your business that you should not be leaving for others to manage and make decisions about? What are your hesitations?
6. How do you rate your multitasking and micromanaging skills? What can you do to enhance those skillsets?

Don't Be So Sensitive.
Tough It Out, Snowflake!

We have raised a generation of "snowflakes," people who give too much credence and importance to relatively minor slights. Overly sensitive. Defensive. Easily offended by trivial provocations. Superficial to the point of "me first, you second, but maybe, only if I have time for you, or if I have the inclination to shift attention away from me."

So, who says that's all bad? Did I make it sound like shortcomings? In business, it certainly is not. It's called "survival." But there is a dangerous tendency to overdo it; letting this "prince or princess" attitude affect your business decision making, and that's bad.

In the old days of childrearing, when the chasm between parents and children was very deep, punishment for misdeeds was swift. In school, the strap or ruler was the chosen tool of maintaining discipline. Well, those days are behind us. The pendulum has definitely swung the other way. Too far, actually. We have gone soft and selfish.

You were likely raised with "choices," just as you continue the process with your own kids. The concept of black and white thinking has given way to infinite shades of gray. That applies equally to how you react to people and situations to the point that, in business, you may often interpret constructive, legitimate criticism as personal attacks.

Emotions create blinders. The result is a shift from logic to emotion in how you plan or run your business.

- The business owner, who becomes everybody's best friend, likes to be adored, that is, until situations require making decisions about your "friends" at your work. Turmoil.
- Detesting the gregarious investor (or client) at the meeting, you know, the one you need but cannot show much respect to, has consequences. They offend your sensibilities. Well,

tough. They are the ones you need. Their money pays your Tesla lease costs. Remember that.

- The real-world perspective is not gleaned from Facebook, Twitter, or any other social media. There is life beyond the laptop screen or cellphone. Get out more.
- Apathy and hypersensitivity are the two extremes of today's society. Don't dwell at either pole.

A major U.S. university attempted a social experiment. Not wanting to hurt anyone's feelings, it was decided that nobody would fail a course. Marks were scored as "I can see you trying" or "Improvement necessary." The results? Competition came to a standstill. The will to win disappeared. Students coasted. Graduates were ill-prepared to face life beyond the womb of academia. We have grown soft, sensitive, and susceptible.

I have dealt with wealthy morons and obnoxious power people, some with success, others not so much. In some situations, the trigger between "business road rage" and "teary regret" has been hairline. Emotions front and center.

In one case, I was invited to the auspicious CFO offices of a multinational. The CFO was condescending from the moment he limply and oh-so reluctantly took my outstretched hand. I was a gnat he needed to but didn't want to have to deal with. The situation was on the path toward unbearable, but my tactic was simple. Grin and bear it.

He wanted a quote for my company's consulting services right there at our meeting. I stalled in an effort to learn more about his needs and expectations, all of which were explained with patronizing indignation. I would not make a decision based on irrational or emotional thinking. The more he pushed, the more I fumed inside, and the higher the fee structure grew in my own mind. I also felt he was the kind who related high cost to quality, that is, the "snob appeal syndrome."

I genuinely felt that, somehow, he felt sorry for me. I hated being looked down upon. See? Emotions!

When it came time to quote our fees, I cited a ridiculously high figure, about 3 to 4 times what I would normally have proposed. This was also my way of getting even, but with a "toughened up" attitude. The contract was mine. I played into his empathy. He needed to reward the peasant.

Here's another quick example. I had a barista get mad at me once because I didn't say thank you pleasantly enough. "Look," said I, "I don't want a relationship with you, I just want a frigging coffee!" I even added "please." He refused to serve me and said I was too rude. Obviously, a graduate of today's overly sensitive, defensive generation.

Business calls for clear-headed thinking. Emotions aside, there is no place for pity-me attitudes or personal likes or dislikes. Business is business. Toughen up, Snowflake. Or, in the words of my eight-year-old granddaughter, "Suck it up, buttercup."

Workbook

Answer true or false to these statements; then expand your response justifying your choice.

1. It is right to reject work because I don't like the client.
2. I tend to make emotional decisions in business.
3. I get offended by people in business whom I do not like.
4. I am affected by other people's moods.
5. I am self-conscious in meetings and networking situations.
6. I am insulted personally when I lose in business.
7. I sometimes make business decisions out of anger.
8. I tend to seek out positive reinforcement.

If you answered "true" to five or more of these questions, you need to take a serious look at how to separate sensitivity from your business tools.

Seriously, it's time to toughen up.

The Happiness Factor

Without being happy, you will be firmly imbedded in the quicksand of somewhere between apathy and "I don't really want to do this"/"Why am I doing this?"/"I'm not having any fun."

Happiness in business is one of those soft, squishy, tough to define personal things that we talk about, but never seem to get our arms around. Yet it is one of the most impactful elements that influence the success or failure of your business. So, let's actually define it.

You need to be happy with what you are doing. That translates to being comfortable, driven, proud, motivated and, yes, even inspired. Ecstatic is a rarity. Happiness actually applies to business as much as it applies to just about anything in life.

Frank (a former client) had built a moderately successful business that he considered "good enough," meaning that it had reasonable opportunities for growth, but he seemed indifferent to follow through on any of the expansion game plans we developed for him. As I got to know him better, I understood his predicament.

He went into business as a necessity, not out of desire. He had been laid off and needed to find a job. He chose entrepreneurship as a way to buy himself one. His other motivation was to appease his life partner who was using Frank as a vehicle for their own ambition. Home life was an unhappy place, and this translated directly to his business. Two strikes.

Even hiring us to develop growth strategies was a feeble effort by Frank to placate his partner. Our presence was lip service. Strike three.

Eventually, both of Frank's relationships, business and personal, failed, but he took it all in stride. In fact, he seemed happier. Relieved and unburdened. And I gained the perspective that business was not just numbers and markets and bottom line. It was about needing to be happy, defined as not being unhappy. It's all a matter of degrees.

Think of business as the equivalent of building a relationship with a (hopefully) exciting and vibrant life-partner who recognizes your abilities, and buys into your business vision. They are there for you as much as you are obsessed with pleasing them and fulfilling their image of you as a successful entrepreneur. (This is just an analogy, and not a marriage proposal.)

Personally, I have always loved the business world, and whatever venture I had built for myself. I maintained a balance of work, family, and home, and that fueled me to continue on my business journey every day. There was (and is) equilibrium in my life.

Now picture an opposite scenario. Every day is somewhat of a chore. Everything you do has elements of "why bother" as you drag the millstone of dispassion behind you. Chances are you are good and stuck, heading toward the quicksand, possibly even intentionally maneuvering your business toward its demise. Is there a smidgen of relief when you envision that? Get out, or change...and change is very much an option. Here's how.

1. Don't go it alone. Find a mentor or life partner who shares your definition of success.

2. Do a "state of mind" reflection before you launch, or if you have arrived at a crossroads in your existing business. Are you ready to move forward? If not, think about what the real or perceived roadblocks are, and if they can (or even should) be breached.

3. Create a Plan "B," a safety net in case things don't work out. That in itself will give you comfort.

4. Establish a "red line" to delineate what you can or are willing to endure in business. That could be "hard stuff" such as financial or burgeoning risk levels, or "soft stuff," defined as impactful personal limits including stress, family, relationships. Maybe it's just a discomfiting state of mind.

5. Speak to others. If you feel you have surpassed the euphoria of business and started wandering listlessly into the grind, then do something. Recognize the business and personal dangers, and take action. Is your passion still there?

6. Your conscious acts as your safety net. It will sound the alarm, sometimes subtle, other times like a wild animal stuck in a trap. Pay attention.

Maybe all of this chapter is for naught, and you are a happy, contented entrepreneur with a song in your heart and a life partner who belts out the same tune. That is awesome.

But if that is not the case, if there are business roadblocks or challenges you simply don't want to face, or any other discord in your life impacting your ability or interest to act, then step aside and assess, or walk away.

Life is too short to tow a backbreaking or mind-numbing burden. Get happy.

Workbook

1. List five things that make you happy.
   - Are they working for you?
   - Anything you need to do to make yourself happier?
2. List five things that make you unhappy.
   - Are they real or perceived?
   - Is there corrective action you need to take?
3. If you could redirect your business to make yourself happier, what would that look like? List five items:
   - Are they doable?
   - How would they impact your business happiness?

What to Do When Nobody Loves You

In life, when we say nobody loves you, it implies it's a lonely, anxiety-producing, depressing, and generally super negative time. You feel abandoned. Ignored. Despair sets in. You feel unworthy. Your emotions are raw from anguish. You are trapped in a downward spiral of self-loathing. Well, guess what? In business, it's exactly the same, but it's hardly fatal. It's an opportunity to springboard back and recapture your prominence as the homecoming queen (or king).

Meanwhile, you are good and stuck. The phone stops ringing. E-mails are mostly about Russian women seeking companionship. Your followers on social media have sought out greener pastures. Your salespeople are perfecting their Wordle or Sudoku. Calls from your banker are becoming too frequent.

You have been abandoned for a reason. Let's find out why, and rekindle the vision and motivation that got you into business in the first place. It's there, just beyond your outstretched grasp, but close enough that, with some introspection, change of attitude and action, you can claw back what you have lost, or have simply misplaced. That's all it might be; disrupted, misfired success.

So, as one option, you can spend some time with a personal guru. Meditate. Connect with your inner you. Let the sanctity of selflessness free your burdens. Levitate. Take a drive through the highways of your mind. (But remember to pack spare gas cans.)

Or, alternatively, just deal with it. Here's how.

- Determine if it's just you. Has your life been disrupted by something unsettling? Family issues? Relationship gone bad? You need to keep those worlds apart. They are often incompatible, each striving to be the alpha.

- If you are distracted by other opportunities, think how your balancing act is damaging all the balls being juggled. You are great, but even the great are limited to 24-hour days. Let something drop for now.

- Did your business simply get boring? Same old same old products, services, marketing strategies? Same messages being regurgitated and spewed out? Repackage yourself. Shake the complacency. Try edgy stuff to get found by those whom you lost. You might try guerilla marketing; affordable, fun, and often very effective.

- Perhaps you, Mr. Reliable, are no longer interesting, or have worn out your market welcome. Find ways to get noticed, personally. Become more rebellious but not noxious.

- Get proactive in reaching out to your customers, motivating your staff, and being a leader who inspires.

- Who's your target market? Not the ones you appealed to years ago, but now! All those baby boomers you sold to get boomed? Find out and refocus, from your packaging and branding to your attitude. Realign your stuff to your current market.

- Are you selling something people still want? Obviously not so much. Find out what the market needs. Do lots of "market research." Do it now, and repeat it regularly. Don't let obsolescence creep up on you.

- Which competitors are doing well? Why? Possibly borrow some of their glitz, or ride on their coattails of success. Get noticed.

- Is location a selling feature for your company? If so, has the neighborhood changed? If you are a destination, can customers still find you?

- Find people who can help; driving traffic to your website; setting up regular blogs; marketing campaigns; better customer followup; product and/or service redevelopment. Delegate. Rely on the expertise of others. Stop doing everything yourself. It's not working for you.

- Hire fresh blood. Let them become the new "face" of the business. You've brought your business to where you are now. Now, let others help advance it several stages forward.
- Find out what your customers/clients like or dislike and need or want. Ask them. Carry out surveys and seek out customer feedback. Show them you care.
- Incentivize your customers. Find ways or develop programs that give something back instead of always taking. People like freebies, gifts, discount packages, free consultations, and referral fees.

These are some of the best strategies to consider. They are defined as approaches that can deliver change; for you and your business.

Alternatively, as suggested earlier, you can become or stay despondent, or simply chose to ignore the need to change, and take that divine pathway to inner peace...and the grim hardships of the quicksand pit.

Workbook

Taking all of the comments and "what ifs" listed in this chapter, carry out the following.

1. Do you have a viable business? How do you know? List the top reasons that you know your business is still viable and competitive.
   - Anything need changing/tweaking?
   - Can you prove it to yourself?
2. Do some soul-searching. List out five things as to why you personally might be failing to impress others. Now think about how you can change.
3. Do the same for your business.
4. Develop an outline for a "Game Plan for Change" for both your business and for you as it's undauntable leader.
5. What has changed in the marketplace? Technology? Competitors?
   - Target markets? How can you change to fit the new marketplace parameters?

What You Are Doing Today You May Not Be Doing Tomorrow

One of the great anomalies in business is that companies, particularly stuck ones, will often end up doing something totally different from what they are doing today. Companies evolve and change. This is a certainty for all entrepreneurs. This concept can sound very cerebral but it's natural and it just happens. Too often we are so ensconced in what we are doing today that we miss the chance to do something better.

How you respond to uncertain circumstances and unanticipated events is critical to your future business success. What happens when a crisis arrives and upends your business? What do leaders do when uncertainty disrupts their existing knowledge and experience? They react.

No planning or preordained strategy can explain this. You can be sure that it will happen to you and you constantly need to be on the lookout for it. The trick here is to be ready and open to recognize it as it tends to pass you in the night.

I was once preparing for a major pitch to a big retail chain that I had targeted as a potential outlet for our product. As part of my pitch to them, I had used our very sophisticated analysis techniques to determine which stores would be particularly successful in selling our product. This analysis included a vast number of variables that made up our algorithm. The sole purpose of this analysis was to show the chain's management that our product would be a successful addition to their offering.

The meeting was a big success and we got the contract. As the meeting broke up, the president of the chain cornered me and asked me to join him in his office. This mini meeting turned into an astounding opportunity.

Our algorithm had selected their best stores by sales and he was totally focused on how we accomplished that, and more importantly, how could he get access to our process. Instantly a new business was created.

What was designed as an internal process for us became a "service" that we could sell to an industry. Wham, within seconds we had evolved from a product wholesaler into a systems provider with a key customer.

Don't let traditional thinking overpower your creative ability to jump on change. Business studies refer to this state of readiness as competing types of knowledge:

- *Explicit Knowledge* is made up of your experiences, training, and education. It is more traditional.
- *Tacit Knowledge* is more subjective and creative and is often referred to as "knowing why." It has an ethereal nature.

Agile leadership is the ability to harness your tacit knowledge and re-examine your assumptions; throw out the current baggage that isn't working and invent a new solution. How you respond to newfound opportunities, uncertainty, and unanticipated events is critical to your business success.

Workbook

1. Make a list of 10 things that will push you outside your comfort zone including five possible setbacks and five potential opportunities.
2. What action would you take for each one?
3. If your strategy is inaction, what would be the costs and damages incurred?
4. Opportunities squandered?

Fear of Networking

Does every chance you get at networking for a connection or business lead turn into an anxiety attack? You hate it? You fear it? You are intimidated by? Even though you know full well that you should be joining in, schmoozing and trying to look interested, you just hug the bar or buffet table at the get-together until the ordeal is over? Guess what? Welcome to the club.

Most people hate networking, yet it is one of the most important communication tools that entrepreneurs need to learn; maybe not "enjoy it," but certainly "tolerate" it, play the game, and reap the rewards. Yes, the rewards of networking are multifold. But, "stuck" entrepreneurs have a tendency to pull back on networking at the very time it is even more critical.

You don't need to be a pull-string Chatty Cathy Doll (was there ever a Verbose Ken Doll?). And nobody wants to be pegged as that insufferable, smiling "networking guy" who hoovers up business cards and offers up his own to anyone within arms-length striking distance.

Does networking make you feel like a phony? Like you don't really fit in or belong there? You are the imposter? Well, you're not. Once you get past the superficiality of it all, the phoniness that swirls about, and the fact that many of the others have the same dislikes and hang-ups as you about networking, you will learn to be a proficient social animal.

Develop your own style that works for you. Business will follow. The stream of contacts, potential clients, and business multipliers (lead generators) will be your prize. But there is more.

For the skilled schmoozers, networking often forges relationships that last well beyond the event. If you are fortunate, you will meet people worth knowing. They may not be useful to you today, but down the road, they can deliver for you, and vice versa.

As well, networking gives you the opportunity to show others that you are someone worth knowing. So, here's how to build confidence and get past feeling like an intruder.

1. Practice, practice, practice. Go to events of minor significance so, when you mess up, or melt away, the damage will be minimal. Learn from your performance.
2. Develop an "elevator pitch," that is, a two-minute storyline of who you are, what you do, and a little smattering of interesting, empathy-generating personal stuff too. Practice your delivery.
3. Create a style you are comfortable with. Your clothes, your attitude, your (maybe real?) confidence. It must be a style you can maintain over the course of the event.
4. Learn to listen. Let others pitch. You catch. Don't worry. You will get your turn.
5. Learn to ask questions, as mundane as some might be. Demonstrate perceived genuine interest.
6. Don't offer up your business card until others offer you theirs.
7. Try to leave the hen-cluster with actionable items, for example, "This is interesting. Let's meet next Friday and talk about this some more."

At any networking event, you are both the predator and the bait. Get used to this dual role.

I had a partner who, as a partner, was unbearable (yes, I am a slow learner sometimes), but as a networker, he was magic. He could join in seamlessly into any group conversation. He could steer the discussion to his own interests. He came across knowledgeable, likeable, and approachable.

On one occasion, I attended two networking events attended by the usual crowd. I was a guest speaker at both. One (brilliant) speech was well received but little after-party networking. Interspersed in the other speech, I happen to drop a number of names. Impressive types. I was literally mobbed afterwards.

This was, by no means, an intentional social experiment. But was this coincidence, or does it prove my point that opportunity-seekers are attracted to other networkers who can dole out happiness? You decide.

Networking does not come naturally to most people. To some it is a disabling prospect. To the introverts and unconfident, it can be a harrowing experience. But it is very much a learned skill bolstered with practice and successes achieved.

Look on networking as an opportunity and enjoy the learning process. After all, what's the worst that can happen if you mess up a few times until you get it right? Absolutely nothing.

Workbook

1. Develop a two-minute elevator pitch that has four components; your product name (service) and what you do; the problems it tackles and benefits it delivers; how this can apply to the person you are speaking with; and schedule an actionable meet up. If you have time, include a little name-dropping too.

2. What are your company's strongest selling points? List them. Learn them. Practice selling them like you mean it.

3. Research others' networking pitches. There are tons on Google and YouTube. Find some that you like and can adopt. List what you like about them.

4. Let a business or company associate pitch to you and see how it feels to be the recipient, or bait. Identify what works. The pitch "hot buttons" create action. List what you did not like about the experience to make sure it does not worm its way into your own delivery.

Guanxi—The Chinese Godfather of Swapping Favors (and Lies)

Western networking is a pretty casual affair. You swap business cards or collaborate on a deal. You go for drinks or dinner, and you may follow up occasionally on social media, with contact lessening over time. It tends to be selfish/self-serving in nature, with parties always seeking favors, but often forgetting to reciprocate. Most western business people correlate networking with "using others," when, in truth, it can be so much more.

Networking is a vital entrepreneurial activity and a skillset that needs to be nurtured. If your networking consists of continually connecting with the same core of people in your tight, little circle, approaching the same multipliers for leads, and your ability to build new long-term business relationships has dried up, then you are clearly "stuck." It's time for you to learn from a culture that has practically invented networking.

Guanxi ("gwan-shi") is an Asian business social currency where you pay and get paid back in favors. It is a relationship built over time and spans decades of parties doing business together. It is a bond that is only as strong as the mutuality of the relationship.

- Guanxi epitomizes the basic dynamic in personalized networks of influence. It can be the key needed to open doors that may otherwise be closed.
- It exemplifies a personal connection between two people in which one is able to prevail upon another to perform a favor or service.
- Reciprocal favors are the key factor in maintaining one's Guanxi web. Failure to reciprocate is considered an unforgivable offense. The more you ask of someone the more you owe them. Guanxi can perpetuate a never-ending cycle of favors.

- It also demands that both parties maintain "face," which is saving their prestige and dignity, and avoiding embarrassment. That includes boasting about wealth and power and embellishing their position in society. That is where the lying comes in. This is where Guanxi parallels western networking. Fluffing up our peacock feathers.
- This relationship is not simply between companies but also between individuals on a personal level. It is like being friends, and friends can count on each other in good and tough times.
- Frequent contact fosters friendship as well. Chinese feel obligated to do business with their friends first. Trustworthiness, business-wise and personal, are important components. Following through on promises is expected.

In one of my ventures, I had started importing ceramic tiles from China. The samples were brilliant. The container loads that followed, however, were pretty abysmal; broken tiles, inconsistent tile finishes, short shipments, you name it.

All the e-mails back and forth were polite but pretty inconclusive. I was getting nowhere. This was odd because the manufacturer had an excellent reputation.

I hired a quality control company in China who were to spot-check production and packaging. The results were only marginally better. They reported that they were shown what the manufacturer wanted them to see, and little more. I decided that this needed more of a personal touch.

I flew over and met with the owners. It was a family business and I met them all. We talked. We dined. We drank (and drank). I offered to introduce them to other North American distributors. We developed some semblance of Guanxi in the process.

My container shipments thereafter began arriving perfectly loaded and with tiles that exceeded my expectations. And once in a while, there was an extra pallet or two for us. Especially after we sent them gifts for Chinese New Year.

It works. Learn to make it work for you.

Let's look at some major differences between Asian Guanxi and western networking. Ask yourself, why can't we integrate more features of

Guanxi into our own experiences? They work, so why not adopt some of them? They can be useful stuck-avoidance strategies.

Guanxi	Western-Style Networking
Develops as a social interaction that translates into business relationships. Business is an extension of the social currency.	Based on the professional level of doing business and rarely built on nurturing a long-term relationship in advance of any networking hook-ups.
There is a strong element of trust. People like doing business with others they trust.	Does greed count as trust? Probably not. Western networkers are always seeking some advantage, gaining clients or getting contacts.
Guanxi thrives on friendship.	Friendship thrives on need.
Guanxi develops and matures over time.	Western networking is built on instant gratification. A very Western trait, unfortunately. Short-term thinking.
Introductions to third parties is taken as a personal obligation by the host.	There is no degree of responsibility by the person making the introductions beyond facilitating the connection.
If one of the party's experiences business difficulties, they may seek out the assistance of their Guanxi counterpart who may feel obligated to help.	Western businesses in trouble will traditionally seek out business consultants, buyers, reorg trustees, liquidators, auctioneers, and vulture capital investors. Doesn't sound as good as Guanxi!

Years back, I started a Networking Club. With about two hundred business members, we extolled the virtues of Guanxi and promoted the mutuality and relationship-building features of effective networking. For members, it proved highly rewarding from both the personal and business perspectives and a learning experience.

Later, while doing business in China promoting my outdoors adventure TV series and working with a major media network of 490 million viewers, I became part of the network's business family. I was adopted. I realized then how our western "hit-and-run" networking had its limitations and could be enhanced by taking a step back to see how business and personal relationships can be more fruitful.

The lessons that can be taken away here is that Guanxi can be applied to your everyday networking and contact-building efforts. It not only delivers opportunities for your business, but it can act as a safety net should you veer off course, get stuck, and need some business friends.

Workbook

1. List the top five deliverables you expect out of any networking situation.
2. Create a chart with two columns. The left column lists business contacts. The right column list business friends. Any shortfalls?
3. List five expectations you might have from your business contacts.
   - What could you offer them in exchange?
4. If your business gets stuck, or engulfed in quicksand, who would you turn to? Can you name five business friends who could help?

Boot These Words and Phrases From Your Business-Speak

Words can be traps, so choose yours carefully. In business, the wrong words can jumble your intended message. Their too-often-misinterpreted innuendos play a significant role in how you are perceived and whether or not you are worthy of doing business with them.

The words you use in your business dealings can place you in a certain era with which you may or may not want to be pigeon-holed. "That's cool" places you squarely into the seventies, while "holistic" identifies you as a relative newbie, almost a business fetus.

The English language has 470,000 words (Oxford and Webster Dictionaries), so I am sure you can find alternatives to this hoard of cringe-worthy words that are just not "cool" to sling around.

Here is a choice handful of my favorite (sic!) outlaw words and the dangerous misperceptions they can generate ("What Others Might Hear"). As a balance, this chart also includes better alternatives you can substitute for these outliers ("Acceptable Alternatives").

Outlaw Word	What Others Might Hear	Acceptable Alternative
HINDSIGHT	Can infer to others that you messed up somehow and are now likely in the process of trying to salvage a relationship with a customer. "In hindsight, we underestimated the impact of…"	We can learn from the past. Let's take a walk-through.
MUTUAL	What can be interpreted as being in everyone's interest is really you proposing something that benefits your business, first and foremost, and others know it. Business is "me first," and "mutual" can often pretend otherwise.	Both of us need to benefit. Otherwise nobody wins.

(Continues)

(*Continued*)

Outlaw Word	What Others Might Hear	Acceptable Alternative
WIN-WIN	This is another version of "mutual" where people recognize that your first priority is to "win" for yourself, and there may be some trickle down "win" for them.	If you win, I win. Let's talk.
SOLUTION	Likely one of the most overused and insidious terms. "We at Bathroom Solutions offer…": it infers that there is a problem that only you can resolve. It's borderline insulting.	Every challenge or problem has a fix. Let's find it.
BEST or BIGGEST or FASTEST	In the western ideal of superlatives, this genre of words has become meaningless, and using any of them is a turnoff. A big turnoff. The biggest!!!! Especially when you use a multitude of exclamation marks!!!!	We've been told that we are pretty good. (Modesty always works.)
HONESTLY or THE TRUTH BE TOLD	Why are you suddenly honest and truthful? What I hear is that everything you have told me so far is not true.	Let's touch on the downside (and risks). It's also important.
JUST or IT'S JUST THAT	You are skating. This is also often understood as an excuse as to why you have fallen short.	Sometimes we need to talk about what none of us want to hear.
HOLISTIC	This is one of those terms that has made its way over from the "interconnect nature of being" thinking. In business, when I hear it, there is sitar music strumming in the background and little else. Keep it for your yoga classes.	There are a number of facets here that impact upon one another.
CAPITALIZE	In today's age of "mutuality," capitalize makes you come off as a robber baron of days gone by. It has strong selfish connotations.	You can win by taking advantage of this. We'll show you how.
TEAMWORK	It was explained to me by a would-be client that when I said "teamwork," it meant that after the sale was made, I would likely delegate the work to juniors in my company and disappear. It can be seen as acutely offensive, plus your fees are often put in question.	I have a team working with me, but I handle the project personally. I am your key contact.
SORRY	Never, ever say you are sorry, even if you are. Focus on the fix rather than the reason for being regretful.	Let's fix what might have gone sideways.

Outlaw Word	What Others Might Hear	Acceptable Alternative
MISSION STATEMENT	It's a "marketing buzz"; how you want others to think of your company. "We aim to deliver the highest quality … blah, blah, blah." Nobody really takes these seriously, so why spout them?	Yes, we have a mission statement, but what we really stand for is delivering.
OPEN-ENDED	Everything is finite. When I hear this, the implication is that you may have no idea about completing the mandate or work, either from a timeline or budget basis.	Here's the proposed completion date, but let's put in a provision for an xx% timeline overrun, something we can all live with.
REVISIT	Often interpreted as we need to revisit because we missed something the first time around. Not good. Does not instill confidence.	Let's review to make sure we didn't skip over anything critical.
TOUCH BASE	I will get to it when I get to it and will be in touch. Sounds like a "kiss-off" to me.	How about we set up a follow up meeting (or Zoom)?
AT THE END OF THE DAY	It's an ineffective wind-up. I'm tired and I want to leave. Now. Right now.	This is what the end results should look like.

There are so many more, including (but not limited to) the few choice examples listed below.

Tolerance	Brainstorm	ASAP
Forgiveness	Monetize	Culture
Expectations	Impactful	Unpack
Carrot	Motherhood	Synergize
Absolutely	Actionable	Allowance
Proactive	Realizable	Manipulate

The lesson here is to think of the often-subtle implications behind every word or phrase you use in dealing with clients, designing promotional materials, pitching your company or project, or presenting to funders and investors. Don't take language for granted. Your message may not be what is heard by others, and you may never realize where and how you have met resistance or gotten stuck.

And while we're at it, let's offer up a number of hollow, kitschy buzz phrases that make people wince and are also worth eliminating from your business-speak.

Paradigm Shift	Outside the Box	Been There, Done That
On My Radar	The New Normal	Your Money's Worth
Sacred Cow	Agree to Disagree	Of One Mind
Raise the Bar	It Is What It Is	Best Case/Worst Case

Workbook

1. List 10 expressions or phrases you use often in business.
2. Ask your staff or business associates what meaning they apply to them and how they are perceived by others.
3. Go through your promotional materials, website, social media posts, and even PowerPoints that you may use regularly. Identify any words or phrases that can have double or alternate meaning.
4. Think of the alternatives you could use to replace the problematic words or phrases. What might they be and how much more effective/pointed are they? Ask others for feedback.

Old Habits Unfortunately Die Hard

Change is not the enemy of business. Stagnation is.

Clinging to old, entrenched work habits and attitudes long past their "best before" dates is often the mainstay of the stuck entrepreneur; a misplaced allegiance to convenience and comfort. Ultimately, it is also a huge detriment to the business.

The stuck entrepreneur takes pleasure in repetition focused on carrying on in today's ever-changing business environment but framed in yesterday's mindset. The critical ability to adapt, change, and compete effectively is often handicapped.

My father-in-law once told me, as he observed my wife and I interact and play with our young children, "I used to think that for kids up to six, it was our job just to feed them and keep them safe. Nothing more. No play. Nothing emotional. Now that I watch you both and see what I missed out on. I wish I had the chance to relive those years with you."

Habits operate on autopilot. It's time to set a new flight path.

The stuck entrepreneur can embrace a new perspective on how to deal with people, business challenges, and opportunities. By identifying bad (and good) habits (see the chart that follows), the stuck businessperson can understand the need for change. It's a personal decision, really, as to how far to undertake the transformation. However, we are in a period of enlightenment. So, enlighten!

Habits and Attitudes of the Stuck Versus the Unstuck Businessperson

The Stuck Entrepreneur

Ownership can undermine your need to strategically plan for the long term. "I am in charge. I know what I need to know." Even mismanaging your day-to-day time.

Not putting aside time off for switching off; overimmersed in your business at the expense of health and family.

Less importance in addressing employee turnovers. Ignoring the warning signs of discontent.

Possibly taking customers for granted, even though 80 percent of your business comes from 20 percent of your customers.

Doing business with friends and relatives is a formula for disaster. So is hiring them. But you do it anyway.

Stuck entrepreneurs tend to be perfectionists often to the point that nothing is ever ready. Missing markets and opportunities and allowing competitors to leapfrog you are the potential downsides.

Inability or unwillingness to delegate, coupled with the need to <u>over</u> micromanage. This is a dangerous time-and-attention-heavy duo. Toxic multitasking is a given, even when it shouldn't be part of your character. It's insecurity. You just don't let things go.

The "blame game." Stuck businesspeople are often reluctant to accept blame for their actions or inactions. It's always someone else's fault. (Politicians have perfected this. LOL)

The stubborn streak; an impenetrable "moat of intractability" encircling you.

Researching markets is secondary to your self-proclaimed ability to understand what others are missing. Why bother, right? (Wrong!)

Finally, quitting when things go awry. After all, none of this is your doing, right?

The Unstuck Entrepreneur

Loves (or at least, really likes) work, thrives on teamwork and comradery, and the corporate culture they have developed.

Seeks out mentors and counsel from others they recognize as smarter or more successful than themselves.

Understands that they do not have all the answers but know where they can find them.

Common sense is not that common but more prevalent among the unstuck.

Miracle fixes and gold-lined opportunities are recognized for what little they are worth.

Some are showboats, but most are introverts who just get stuff done. They seldom self-promote and gain satisfaction from what they have created. They are secure.

Rarely involve family in the business, except if they bring them in at low-end positions and encourage them to learn and work their way up the corporate hierarchy.

> ### Habits and Attitudes of the Stuck Versus the Unstuck Businessperson
>
> Almost perfectionists but with a strong sense of timing. Sometimes good enough is good enough.
>
> Gathers as much information, insight, and current research as they can. Market research and preparedness are keys. Avoids knee-jerk instinctual reactions.
>
> Surrounds themselves with people who can share the decision making.
>
> The unstuck businessperson takes the hit for their errors. They are leaders and accountability is their responsibility.
>
> Change and adapting to change are the first options, well ahead of quitting and finger-pointing.

Now that we have presented a basic snapshot of wrong and right habits, hopefully you recognize where there may be room for improving your playbook of possible mindset and performance obsessions.

Workbook

1. Acknowledge and list your intransigent behavior. If you are not sure, ask those around you. They will gladly share their observations with you. You can even make a contest or game out of it to get people to open up about you.
2. Try to identify where these issues come from. That will help you deal with and alter them.
3. For the top five old habits you have identified, list the steps you might take for changing them. Prepare an action plan to dump those old habits and replace them with "new, improved" behavior.
4. Do you expect others to work at your pace? That may be an annoying hold-over habit and a source of conflict for you. List the last five times you "lost it" over someone's work or timing, or whatever event triggered it, and ask yourself "Was I overreaching with my expectations?" Take your findings to heart.
5. Within six months, start to track the results of your makeover. Less staff turnover? Better team performance? Increased orders and sales/contracts? Now, keep tracking that trend every six months and act on the findings.

Learn From My Mistakes

We are told time and again, and again, to learn from our mistakes in business so that we do not repeat them. Yet the reality is that not only do we often replicate our blunders, but the act of doing so actually reinforces our bad behavior. Costly decisions. Gaffes. Stuck in a cycle of lapses we now misconstrue as proper learned responses.

As put succinctly by Peter Cook and Dudley Moore in a comedic skit:

Have you learned from your mistakes?
Yes, I have. And I am confident that, if asked, I could repeat them all perfectly.

Our human nature defense-mechanism steadfastly tells each of us to hold ourselves and our actions in the highest self-regard. That protects our egos, but not our outcomes. We pay little attention to the equally valuable but cast-off lesson(s) we can profit from when we do mess up. That is naïve, bordering on sometimes-fatal narcissism.

And it's not just our own blunders. Chances are, whatever mistakes you have made, or about to make, have already been done by someone out there who has recognized and journalized their failing. Others have beaten their heads on the wall. Learn from them.

Why can't you learn from my mistakes? It will take you half a lifetime to make your own.
—*A Taste of Honey* Movie, 1961.

In my first partnership, I was barely a fertilized business embryo. Greed and cash flow needs obscured my reasoning. I turned a blind eye to what should have been red flags and, instead, allowed myself to be painted into a corner by my partner's wealth, his family prominence, and his lawyer's partnership agreement. That's correct, I even allowed his lawyer to dictate the inequitable working relationship. I worked, he shared the profits without delivering what he had promised to. It ended badly. I spent more time infighting than generating revenues. Quite the lesson.

For my second partnership, I revisited all my scars from before. I researched other successful and failed partnerships to determine how to make them work and what to sidestep. I used my own first partnership's red flags to build a strong working partnership that survived and succeeded for years.

So, in the "live and learn" category, you will likely make mistakes in your career. Just don't get stuck repeating them, and learn from others who have already paid the price.

Learn from the mistakes of others. You can't live long enough to make them all yourself.

—Eleanor Roosevelt.

Here's how to buddy-up with mistakes, yours and others. These strategies will help you be a better-rounded businessperson and may well get you out of "stuck-inducing" situations.

1. Don't just idolize and role model the successful players. Look beyond the tinsel and glitzy wrappings. When you research, seek out the dirt too that helped shape their careers.

2. Research and then research more. There's plenty of material out there. While some businesspeople/authors write about their successes, there are almost as many who invite you to wallow in their failures and shortcomings. It has become chic to open up and share.

3. Every experience is an adventure. Some are good; others are mistakes. Celebrate the successes but view the failures as simply a hurdle or learning experience.

4. There is no shame in failure, except if failing becomes a repeat performance.

5. Lessons learned in failing are generally relevant to a cross-section of economic sectors and circumstances. Broaden the parameters of your indoctrination.

6. Share experiences with business associates and encourage them to share with you. Use these confidants as sounding boards.

While failure is never a welcome companion, it is part of being in business. Nobody ever sets out to fail, but when it happens, embrace it as a lesson in the school of hard knocks, and move on, better prepared for the next adventure. It makes you tougher and more resilient.

Workbook

Failure in business comes in degrees, from granting excessive credit to a client to launching into a business venture that has a near-term "best before" date.

1. List three such failures of varying significance and impact you have experienced. For each one, generate the following:
   - What did I learn from the mistake(s)?
   - Did I ever repeat the mistake(s) again?
   - In my current business, do I apply these safeguards to pre-serve my operation?
2. List three failures you have witnessed in others, preferably with busi-ness associates you can speak with freely.
   - What did they learn from their mistakes?
   - Did they ever repeat the mistakes again?
   - In their current business, do they apply these safeguards to preserve their operation?

Get Rid of the Guru, Keep the Mentor

Outside business advice is critical to the rebirth and growth of all stuck ventures. It can shape your "go forward" plan and greatly enhance your prospects for success. But be aware; there are useful advisors (mentors), and there are nonadvisors (gurus). For a stuck entrepreneur, there is a vast difference in what they each brings to the table. Too often the roles of business gurus and mentors are either erroneously comingled or confused.

- A mentor's role is to provide you specific advice on your business needs that is based on their own real-world experience. Mentors are usually very supportive of you and your business concept, take an interest in your venture, and focus on specific issues, challenges, and opportunities. Their advice is realizable/implementable.
- A guru's self-aggrandized big picture generic advice is rarely helpful for an entrepreneur's current and critical needs. Gurus tend to pitch staid and elusive formulae for success rather than practical and doable action items. Gurus are often expensive. It is their primary business to take your money.

There is no "one size fits all" formula for entrepreneurial success. You need to pick and choose what works for you. My experience is that entrepreneurs are very individual and unique people, and any idea that they should fit into somebody else's mold is nonsense.

Business is personal. Adopt what others' ideas and mentor strategies work for you, and make them yours.

Why Mentors?

- Mentors listen and deal with your specific vision and situation.
- A mentor's advice is based on extensive first-hand business experience.

- Mentors stick with you as your business evolves.
- Mentors challenge you to deal with issues and opportunities that you have never considered.
- Mentors can open doors that can help your business grow.

Why Not Gurus?

The world of successful business gurus is totally disassociated from the world of entrepreneurism; I call it "the lying kingdom." Here are some of my favorites "guruisms":

- Beware of the "*overnight success*" stories that are out there. Most of them are simply catchy nonsense and are more like the latest diet fad from late night TV.
- "If you have a good idea for a start-up, just go out there and get financed and start your company." If reality was only that easy! I've never met a start-up that could magically finance an idea on day one.
- "Get up at 5 AM every morning and meditate, write in your personal journal and maybe do some yoga to center your mind." I've known a lot of successful entrepreneurs, but I must have missed the ones that followed this regime religiously.
- "Emulate the practices from a list of 'excellent' companies." Unfortunately, time has shown that many of these excellent companies generated really average results. Not much to emulate here.

My most painful guru experiences revolved around a business investor who had gained his vast expertise through multiple stays in posh drug rehab facilities. Fortunately for him, his family amassed considerable wealth while he was on his numerous "vacations."

His investment in our company led to his acting as our corporate guru who graced us by attending several management meetings and offering his blurred visionary slant on the business landscape.

It soon became an inside joke that he actually arrived in town on a magic carpet rather than an airplane. He would lead us in "centering our inner beings" while we tried to focus on the pedestrian stuff like monthly budget reports and production numbers. Needless to say, we all found this very "useful" (not) and soon secretly started referring to him as the (now politically incorrect) Maharishi Yogi Bear.

He would mercifully end his guidance to us just before noon so that he could have lunch in one of the city's most expensive restaurants which he would always bill back us. We always had a good laugh after he left as we got back to the real world of business. No doubt this was where the term "Gurucide" was coined.

I'm not saying that we need to axe all the gurus. It's just that we need to be suspicious of highly dubious advice and get-rich pitches spouted by a group of business pretenders who inhabit the guru stratosphere.

It's time to leave the gurus behind and focus on us, the entrepreneurs. We are members of an exclusive group that includes huge success stories that started small and made their own early missteps. These include Apple, Google, and Amazon.

In actual fact, there are tens of thousands of new ventures that entrepreneurs have launched every year. Most new ventures are not massively disruptive or world changers. They are businesses that are inspired by the passion of the entrepreneurs that champion them. Many of them couple entrepreneurial desire to existing industries. We see examples of this in our own neighborhoods every day:

- There are twice as many independent car dealerships in the United States (entrepreneurs) than there are branded dealerships.
- There are approximately 1 million restaurants in the United States and the majority of these are independent locations (entrepreneurs).

Entrepreneurs are a unique club that generates billions of dollars in revenue and makes the earth turn.

Find the mentor that will help shape your new plan into a reality. Your "moving forward" strategies should be grounded in realizability. Concentrate on the opportunities that you can reach out and touch.

Workbook

1. List the areas that your new plan needs to address.
2. Start a mentor search. What skills are you looking for? Make a "shopping list" of features you expect in a mentor.
3. List your business contacts that can help with your mentor search.
4. Advise your lawyer, accountant, and banker about your needs for a mentor. They are a great source for introductions.
5. Prepare a synopsis of your stuck situation to share with your mentor candidates.
6. Be very precise in your expectations, timelines, milestones, and budget.
7. Interview prospective mentors using the checklist you have prepared. Gage the chemistry between you and the mentors. That is important as well.

Bring Your Personality to the Table

If you were asked "what do you bring to the table in business?" no doubt you would list a plethora of skills, insight, knowledge, and certainly some relevant experience. But chances are your "personality" would not rate very high on your list. That is so wrong. Your personality can dictate your business success, or failure.

A "business personality" is how others see and react to you based on how you see and react to others. It is reciprocal and highly impactful. An effective business personality is a sign of your business and professional maturity. It is power; your weapon to wield in every aspect of your business life.

It influences others' behavior and that includes how they respond to your networking, communications, and even your selling efforts. It is your acting out to gain an expected outcome or advantage. It is control.

However, not all businesspeople have the kind of personalities that work for them. You may be introverted, shy, uncomfortable in your own "business skin," or simply lack what it takes to promote yourself, your company and/or whatever marketing, sales, or investor pitch you may be delivering. Being stuck is debilitating, but not fatal. Toughen up. Here's how.

1. You need to be the instigator, the one who brings out the best in employees, co-workers, and associates by exuding and "oozing" confidence. You inspire and motivate because you want others to consider you a leader and, most importantly, deliver results for you. There is ALWAYS an end goal. Fake it if you need to.
2. Your business personality should be selfish and insatiable, and almost predatory.

3. Be grateful. Showing gratitude is a way to weaken others' defenses. Flattery can be real, or somewhat less authentic, or simply calculated to generate a warm fuzziness that loosens others' resistance.

4. Be outwardly open but only to the point that you are not exposing your vulnerable flank. If you can succeed in making others feel you are divulging something only to them, taking them into your confidence, you can expect something important in return.

5. Practice being sincere. It comes naturally to some but not to everyone. Again, learn to fake it if it is not in your character to ooze sincerity on demand.

6. In my experience, I have learned to be selectively trustful of people, and when someone quips "to tell you the truth," I expect anything but.

7. Be "nice." This is something you hear quite often. Or "play nice." So, adopt a "nice guy" business personality, but the truism has a selfish twist. That is, "be nice to people who can deliver something back to you." The "what's in it for me?" is a crucial factor in the "be nice" scenario. While it's okay to be nice to all, just be selectively nicer if there is something in it for you.

8. Smile, smile, smile. It breaks barriers. This helps develop trust and creates an aura of confidence and assurance. And it costs you nothing.

9. When you are bettered or offended, or have clients or market share poached by a competitor, turn the other cheek. But never forget. And you will have the opportunity for retribution, especially when they are not expecting it.

10. Be outgoing but not obsequious. People like proactive, communicative businesspeople, so try to build that into your personality without coming across like a desperate gouger needing that one more sale to complete your monthly quota. *"A compliment is the stating of a pleasant truth. Flattery is the stating of a pleasant untruth."*

11. Be a friend but only if you can get something in return. Be that amigo when it serves your purpose. Business friendship is a well-travelled two way street.

12. Think of others, only after thinking of you. You are number one. Never lose sight of that. Act only if it is in your best interest.

13. Get into peoples' heads. Understanding the psychology of business provides a formidable weapon and needs to be part of your business personality arsenal.

Workbook

1. Do a chart. On the left side, list 10 things you do in business that can be deemed **selfish**. Then, in the middle column, analyze why you do them and what you get from them. In the far-right column, gage for yourself how they can be bettered, or tweaked, or eliminated if the deliverables are scanty.

10 Selfish Business Acts You Do	Why Do Them, What Benefits Do You Get From Them?	How Can They Be Tweaked Or Eliminated?
1		
2		
3		
4		
5		
6		
7		
8		
9		
10		

2. Repeat the above chart, but list 10 things you do in business that are **unselfish**. What do they get you? How much time do they take? Do they add to your entrepreneurial level of enjoyment?

3. Review the results of the charts and decide what changes you may want to institute, if any.

4. Who are your business heroes? Research their strategies and decision making, and identify the strongest facets of their business personalities. Anything you can learn from that?

5. Research websites, books, and blogs on getting into peoples' heads. There is a great deal of insight you can glean. The entrepreneurial mind is an interesting and rewarding place to hang out. There are numerous books on dissecting the entrepreneurial mind and finding the "hot buttons" that drive people to act. Resources on Business Psychology can provide you with more insight into finding those critical "hot buttons" in others.

Don't Be a Sheep

There are two extreme, polar opposite personalities in business: (1) the power-hungry huckster, and (2) the sheep.

- The **huckster** gets the media attention and an adoring cult that feeds his or her ego, and is generally a master at being Machiavellian, that is, winning at any cost.
- The **sheep**, when confronted or challenged, fades timidly and well "sheepishly" into the shadows of stuckitude; a place where the awe-inspiring is often overshadowed by the ho-hum.

Which one are you? Where do you fit in the spectrum?

Sheep behavior manifests itself in any number of ways, all of which lead the stuck to follow the herd, or keeping to midway or at the back of the pack. Anonymity is a big deal for the sheep.

Perhaps it's time to slough off any lemming-like behavior. People will not think any less of you, and you may be embarking on a new you, an "achiever" instead of an "also-ran."

The loss of opportunities, fear-induced paralysis to act/react, dread of the unknown (and often the known as well), and dwelling in a very narrow comfort zone are but a few of the traits that characterize the sheepish businessperson. Invisibility is not pretty or productive.

But you don't have to be the huckster either. There is a happy medium.

- Don't hang around sheep. Safety in numbers does not justify sheep behavior.
- Stop agreeing with others when your instinct tells you to do otherwise.
- Understand that your opinions and convictions count, regardless of the scowls of those other sheep around you. They are yours. Respect them.

- Plot your own course in business. Take some risks.
- Make others jealous of you.
- Learn to be different. If you don't fit in, then you're probably doing the right thing.

I had a client who developed advanced technology to freeze-dry fruits and vegetables in large quantities without losing any of the nutritional benefits, taste, or texture of the product. My client was the brains behind the technology. Frankly, it was amazing. However, as clever as he was, he was far too sheep-like.

He had a partner/investor who was busy hording the intellectual property and developing a parallel technology as well as a separate production facility. While my client (the nice guy) recognized the thievery, he was reluctant to act. After all, the families summered together at the lake, the wives and kids had bonded, and my client (still the nice guy) was reticent to take action.

I physically had to coach him how to be "meaner," and how to shed his sheepish behavior and stand up for what was his. I helped him lead the legal charge against his partner, but moreso, forced him to take on the role of the proactive aggrieved player.

I prodded and pushed him to act outside his "far-too-nice guy" nature, partly by demonstrating the harm being done to him and his business, and his family.

I correlated "mean" with "just," and that analogy was the one he adopted comfortably.

In the end we won. He won. And he became a far better businessman in the process. But the transition was not easy.

Here is some more advice on how to be meaner, that is, somewhat less "sheep-like."

- Don't worry about what others say. *"A lion never loses sleep over the opinions of sheep."*
- Be firm without being disrespectful. Maintain the high road.
- Stand your ground for what you believe.
- Business is not personal. Don't let emotions get in the way.

- Collaboration is better than conflict, but if that does not work, don't hesitate to act alone and in your own self-interest.
- Always try to figure out the other person's reasoning/motivation and use it to your advantage, or even against them if it fits into the interaction.
- Being meaner in business does not mean being hurtful or cruel. It implies taking and maintaining control.

All of this may well be against your nature, but in business, it is a survival tactic. Perhaps you can think of it as a role you play, a character who is strong without being heartless, and being supremely assertive, but not acting out of pettiness or spite.

Remember the idiom, "nice guys finish last." Don't let yourself get outmaneuvered by others who don't play as nice as you do. Stand up for what you believe and for what you are owed. You are your number one consideration.

Workbook

1. If you ask people to describe you in business, what might they say? List the top 10 responses you get. Anything in there about being "too nice"?
2. Think about this. Where is your "red line" that would get you angry enough to abandon your sheepish thinking and get you to act out? What would it take?
3. Have you ever lost out on anything because you didn't want to rock the boat? What did that cost you in terms of opportunity, time, and possibly damages? Do you see it as a valuable lesson?
4. What business traits would you want to work on, namely, the ones that cost you because of your inaction or timidity? List the top five and what you might do to change.

Selective Empathy, Deliberate Deflection, and Elastic Imperatives

Danger, Will Robinson, Danger

—Robby the Robot in *Lost in Space*

We are entering a territory fraught with controversy and danger. Watch your step.

Businesspeople tend to tiptoe around moral issues and behavior that they have carried from their personal beliefs to business. Be nice. Play fair. Sympathize when someone is down, even a competitor. Wallow in forgiveness when you make a mistake. We have all become so oversensitized that capitalizing on opportunities, usually at someone else's expense, makes us feel like usurpers, undeserving despots, and, well, just really bad people. It ain't so.

- Empathy is for sissies.
- Deflection is a coping strategy to protect your pedestal of authority and power.
- Elastic imperatives implies bending the rules to suit your purpose and needs, influences how you react when your focus is squarely on the prize or when you feel threatened. You act out. Elasticity is a good thing.

While that all sounds pretty contentious, let's examine a number of survival doctrines that you may choose to live by, but only if you want to avoid the quicksand abyss.

Firstly, understand that **selective empathy, deliberate deflection, and elastic imperatives** range from extreme behavior through to moderate and to infinite grades of less severe compromise. You don't need to always be the ogre but nor should you ever be the milksop.

Selective empathy is showing compassion to those who can best serve your interests. Our cutthroat business environment has conditioned us toward "tribalism." We have moved from putting ourselves in others' shoes to targeting what empathy we can muster for people who feed us what we demand; revenues/contracts, team/management performance, and opportunities/business possibilities. Everyone else falls into a lower rung deserving only lip service.

Rightly or not, selective empathy conditions us to see some lives as less valuable than ours. Why waste your time on people who have hurt you in business, or people you just don't like, but might feel sorry for? They may have fallen on hard times, or gotten sick. Ask yourself what this has to do with you. Nothing. It sounds shameless, but business tends to reset your "empathy meter."

Empathy for a cause or charity is similar. It exacts a toll on you. You have no control. You cannot influence it. Whatever you do, however you react, employ selective empathy and move on.

I made the mistake of sitting on the Board of a sick children's charity. It was very worthwhile, and we raised a lot of money, but there was a price to pay. After every Board meeting, my heart burst with empathy listening to stories about the brave kids we were helping. I shed quite a few tears. I guess it wasn't really a mistake; we accomplished a lot. But the price it exacted from me is still part of my soul.

Deflection is a common defense mechanism. In the extreme, it is to blame others rather than accepting criticism or blame for your own actions or inactions. The antithetical position is to become the human pincushion. Neither position is good for you. Both drag you down.

The art of deflection is the ability to walk a fine line between being compassionate and understanding, and being the callous marauder; between being genuine and taking action versus playacting concern or deftly unburdening yourself by skating away.

Now, I am not making any political statements here, but when we talk about deflection, our former U.S. President, Mr. Teflon, set new standards. Regardless of what was thrown at him, be they lawsuits, proof of wrongdoing, witness testimonies, or physical evidence, a simple "No, it wasn't me. It's fake" was all it took to dismiss the transgressions and move on. It was, and still is, an amazing lesson in deflection. And entertaining too.

Skating is the cornerstone tactic of deflection. It implies changing the conversation or introducing distractions to the conversation. Answering a question with a question. Changing the subject. Introducing alternate scenarios or contradictory theories. Offering excuses that carry some degree or marginal semblance of legitimacy. (Kind of sounds like politics.) In short, it's lying but done in a way that is neither terribly harmful nor puts you into a position of incredulity. It's still lying, but let's call it **nimble skating**, and trust me, it will save you on any number of tight spot occasions.

It's human nature to show empathy, take the hit when you do wrong, apologize, and genuflect your way out of problems you have created. Skate away.

Become comfortable with deflecting and skating. You may need to fight your natural impulse.

Think of business behavior as the antithesis, but only if you want to stay out of trouble, even if you created the predicament in the first place.

Workbook

Let's work to define your moral compass. The best way to do this is with another person role-playing as the aggrieved party and you need to respond to each scenario below with (1) the right degree of empathy; (2) how you would propose to deflect blame away; and (3) how you skate away to safety.

The other party would rate you on a scale of the following:

1. Very believable
2. Reasonably credible
3. Questionable responses
4. Self-destructive

Here are the situations in the exercise.

- You missed a deadline to submit a proposal and lost out on a contract.
- You have taken credit for sales generated by others and have not given them enough recognition.
- Your business partner has discovered that you are speaking with a third party about buying your shares but had not mentioned it to them.
- Your bank has asked for your financial statements several times over the last few months. You have not obliged, not wanting to disclose your numbers. You skate.
- You quote a client $5/unit. He knows you have sold to his competitor for $4.25. This is an industry with tight margins. He is livid.

Embellish Freely But Don't Believe Your Own PR

To embellish means to adorn, improve by adding details (real or otherwise) or to exaggerate to make something more exciting or interesting. It is the "little white lie" as you enhance a corporate bio, the efficacy of products or services, or your own personal background and credentials. Can you do that? No? Then you are stuck in a world of normalcy when being better is considered, well, better, and embellishment within reason is an acceptable way of doing business.

There are extremes to be avoided. Working with an overseas business development group, I agreed to allow the company to publish my resume on their website. I gave them some basic bio information, and was then astonished when I read about myself on their site. Suddenly, I was a Doctor of Economic Strategic Thinking (?), had graduated from at least three top U.S. universities, and was a consultant to the highest levels of government (it did not state which). Adding up all my quoted years of experience, I would have been 105 years old. I must say, I looked great for 105!

I immediately insisted they remove me from their website, and became quite disillusioned working with them entirely since I now felt that everything they said on their website was not believable. Rather, it was likely outright lies intended to deceive.

Therein lies the "red line" of exaggeration. Wicked lies are not embellishments. They are just lies.

Embellishment needs to distinguish between finely repackaging reality, and "bullshit." The first is a smart, common strategy, and we see it in promotional materials, marketing/investor pitches, and human resources embellishing both the job and the applicant. Everybody does it to some degree, but the businessperson who has "stuck" tendencies may find this difficult or objectionable, even at the cost of losing out on opportunities.

"Bullshit," however, is just embellishment on drugs.

To that effect, let's look at acceptable versus unacceptable embellishing. Hopefully that will help the inflexible (i.e., stuck) person understand and accept certain limits of creative thinking.

GOOD—Telling someone you like their company and products, even if you don't, I mean, really don't. That is acceptable. No harm done. Simply a way to get potential clients to let their guard down and make you approaching them a warm and fuzzy experience.

BAD—On the other hand, promising to triple the traffic to their website in thirty days, or losing twenty pounds in two weeks (I wish!) are lies, not embellishments. They are relationships built on deceit. They will bite you on your toned behind (possibly yet another embellishment?) very quickly.

GOOD—True story. I owned a nutraceutical products company that produced and sold "Baby Boomer Reboot," a marine phytoplankton, all-natural supplement touted to make the user feel more energetic. Well hyped, but all true. Scientifically sound and without making deceptive promises.

BAD—I had a client in the same sector who, for years, produced "heartdrops" formulated with garlic and other natural goodies. They advertised that if you were having a heart attack, pop one of these pills in your mouth and all chest pains and heart attack symptoms would quickly disappear. I confronted them on this blatant falsehood and warned them that the regulatory people would one day jump all over them. It was dangerous BS. I was ignored and I subsequently dropped them as a client. Soon afterwards, all it took was one more user complaint (no, not by me) and the company was shut down under threat of severe legal sanctions. Don't let embellishments get away from you.

Here is some nonembellished advice for the embellishment-deprived businessperson.

- Presentations, proposals, marketing materials, websites, social media, and even PowerPoints should be embellished with graphics, punchy statements, and audience-friendly attention grabbers. All very legit. You may have heard the expression "let's put some lipstick on that pig"? That refers to showing off/bettering/decorating/making something more attractive but generally without morally questionable deceptive trappings.

- Whenever asked if you can deliver something for a proposed customer, and you believe you can but have not done so in the past, say "yes." Then do it.
- Learn to skate, that is, be elusive.
  - *"Do you have a team?" The answer is yes, but in reality, they are all virtual, contracted as-you-need them people. They are still your team.*
  - *"How long have you been doing this?" "Years," but really mostly as an employee and not as an entrepreneur.*

  I think you get the drift here. No harm done, right?
- Never apologize for your mistakes. Assure the injured party that this is a one-off, even if it is part of your modus operandi. Then fix it for good. Better than you had promised.
- Your product or service will not solve anything; it will work toward solving something. It will not cure anything but reduce the symptoms of whatever. For example, it will not leave the user's skin soft as a baby's duff. It will work to eliminate skin roughness and likely make you feel more vibrant. Get it? If you need to embellish, do it as indirectly-inferred generalities.

The final word of caution is that you mustn't believe your own hype. Embellishments are designed to earn you attention, business, rewards, market presence, and/or brownie points. They are an effective extension of the real world.

Isn't that amazing! (Anything that ends in an exclamation mark is an embellishment. Ignore it.)

Workbook

1. Take one of your proposals or promotional materials and dress it up without any over-the-top claims or assertions. Which do you like better? Which style are you more comfortable with? Which can you live comfortably with?

2. What are the five best things about your company? Now, list them in more glowing terms.

3. Do the same exercise for your products or services.

4. Identify five competitor companies offering similar products or services as you do.

   - How do they present and package themselves compared to you?
   - Any outright fibs or fables?
   - Any ideas worth adopting?

Pretending—The "Jekyll and Hyde" Syndrome

Who you are in business may not be who you are in real life. If you are a stuck entrepreneur, and you are not adept at transitioning between both worlds, the challenge can be trying.

Entrepreneurship often demands that the businessperson takes on a role different to their everyday personality, style, ethical behavior, and even their belief system. For most, this is not a totally radical transformation but rather an adaptive shift in their sensibilities in order to meet the demands of their business persona.

There may or may not be any internal conflict in you fulfilling this character that is key in the development and/or growth of the business. It's a question of achieving comfort.

For many, it represents stretching the boundaries of their comfort zone and can induce anxiety and difficulty in maintaining and projecting the guise. In fact, the posturing can become the norm, and conflicts can arise that manifest themselves in the boardroom and in the home environment.

For the stuck entrepreneur, there are coping strategies. Think "comfort zone" and "balance."

It is absolutely critical that the entrepreneur's guise is within sight of their comfort zone but not entrenched in the totally comfortable. Why? Comfort is often cited as "an enemy of progress."

Comfort can equate to standing still, and that can often mean falling behind. It becomes a balancing act. The individual must resist complacency while adopting and embracing change, all within the limits of their ability to perform and pretend to be someone their business needs them to be. Breaches and cracks in their performance can be costly and damaging.

The crucial balancing act here is (1) understanding who you are; (2) truthfully identifying your fears and hesitancies; (3) clarifying what the business demands of you; and finally, (4) what you are capable of taking on and embracing, but without totally jeopardizing what is most important to you, or losing track of the real you.

There are basically only four personalities in business, and each one dictates an assemblage of performance features. Which one (or ones) are you? Identifying your business type (or types) can help you create the business persona that fits you.

1. **Drivers:** Create momentum, embrace challenges, deal quickly with problems, move faster than the speed of rational decision making, and tend to be big picture planners.
2. **Guardians:** Safety and stability are of paramount importance, very methodical and introverted, risk-adverse.
3. **Integrators:** Natural networkers, relationship-builders, nonconfrontational consensus-builders, highly empathetic.
4. **Pioneers:** The high-visibility risk takers powered on by gut decision making and big-picture dreams.

I once had a partner (yes, yet another one) who exhibited Jekyll and Hyde behavior. He was always on the edge of changing over. On a personal relationship level, he was okay, that is to say, tolerable, but worth remaining wary of. In business, he was a beast. His office (smaller than mine, another point of contention between us) was next to mine.

In meetings with clients, his voice was melodious, confident, and gaggingly sweet. I knew he was in his sales mode.

However, in sessions with staff, he berated and intimidated his team mercilessly.

The continuing problem was that his Jekyll and Hyde transformation lost its boundaries. His home life became intolerable to his family (and several consecutive wives), and get-togethers between him and I always ended in screaming matches.

I even arranged an intervention for him. It did not go well.

Your business is not your life. The totality of all aspects of your life is your life. Be conscious and cautious of what roles you take on, especially the ones far different from your own.

Business can eat its young. The chasm between who you are and who you become cannot EVER be impassable.

Workbook

1. Understand who you are. Carry out a strengths and weaknesses appraisal of what makes you tick.
2. What is important in your life?
3. Truthfully identify your fears and hesitancies.
4. Clarify what your business demands of you; the easy, tough, and almost impossible too.
5. Define what you are capable of taking on and embracing the "dark side" but without totally jeopardizing what is most important to you.

Become the "Go To" and Milk It

Leaders don't just get followed. They get chased.

Part of building your "entrepreneurial persona" is becoming a leader, and that implies that others presume you are knowledgeable and open to sharing tidbits of your expertise. The strategy is that they will seek you out, and you ever-so humbly (?) accept your role as an industry sage, even if you are not quite there yet.

Faking it is actually quite easy. Just spout a few well-researched but not widely known facts, and your followers will purr.

It is critical that the stuck entrepreneur develop the ability to become the "go to" and to milk every opportunity.

The stuck businessperson seems to play catch up…forever. If that's you, here is how to break the cycle.

At any opportunity where you are meeting clients, or potential clients, whether that be at trade fairs, marketing or sales pitches, conferences, networking events, or even one-on-one get-togethers, you need to maintain an aura of competence, know-how, and savvy. This is especially true where what you are called upon to share and that sharing can be beneficial to others' businesses. Share cautiously and selectively.

You become the "go to," and you take full advantage of it. Knowledge is power, and sharing it puts a debt onto the other party (parties) to reciprocate. Actually, it's real or perceived knowledge that solidifies your power.

That translates into more business or contracts for your company, and subtly, you make sure that repayment is extracted. There is no need to overpower. People like dealing with people they trust, and sharing is a proven way to build confidence.

Here's how it works.

1. Make others assume you know, or know where to find out.
2. If you have the answers, share them, but only to a point. Knowledge–sharing needs to be the same as a movie trailer. If you limit it to

a "tickler," you exhibit the ability to respond, share, and help, but you leave yourself the opportunity for a follow-up meeting, at which point you can close a sale/contract/deal. Please remember the end-goal is generating business. Do not lose sight of this deliverable.

3. If you do not know, simply defer to your team. "I have those stats at my office. I will fire them over to you." "I know my people were working on just that. Let me get back to you." Show you are making a real effort. Again, follow-up get-togethers are opportunities to close business or build stronger allegiances.

4. Surround yourself with good people, a team that is able to feed you what you need in the way of follow-up responses with prospects you met earlier.

   I always had a "prep team" to feed me background information when I was to meet important clients; company history, key people, "in the news" stuff too.

5. Maintain a network of "knowers," resources you can turn to. Even if you have to pay them, the return on your investment can be significant.

I rarely enjoyed the to-and-fro of organized networking, but I was pretty good at it. Once, in a fit of boredom, I began to wonder if prospects I followed up with after the event yielded more results (contracts, sales, deals) for my business than the one-timers I chatted with at the event itself.

- I chose five attendees, and in our hen sessions, I responded with everything I knew, leaving nothing on the table.
- I chose another five with the specific intent of "let me get back to you on that" strategy and then followed up within a week. Anything beyond a week seems to dampen any urgency on the other party's need or interest, so that was my cutoff.
- With the follow-up group, my results (contracts, sales, deals) were significantly higher (75 percent) than the placebo group.

This two-stage strategy of (1) the go-to and (2) judicious follow-up has been part of my technique ever since. There is nothing unethical involved in this strategy. Human nature is flexible and moldable. And it is far better to be the "molder" than the "moldee."

Perhaps I need to change this chapter's opening line. It could read as follows.

"Business leaders don't just get followed—they get chased, trusted, and hired."

Workbook

1. List five instances where you met others and shared business insight or advice right there during the encounter.
   - What did YOU get out of those encounters? What price did you exact for sharing?
2. Now, think how you could have stalled/followed up after a week. Would it have made a difference in signing new business?
3. Identify 3–5 business gurus or leaders you deal with, or know about. Does their technique sound familiar to the strategies identified in this chapter?
4. Chose a subject of importance in your industry. Now, practice the "movie trailer" approach to information sharing. Try it out with an associate or two until you perfect it. Gage their response and feedback.
   - Have you generated interest? A willingness to meet again to keep the discussions going?

There is an air of aloofness and detachment in this technique. Don't overdo it. Find a comfortable, workable balance between saint and sinner.

Useful (and Useless) Business Plans

Your Business Plan is dead in the water. Whatever the plan was created to achieve has simply not worked. You don't really know why. No surprise; most probably your style, content, and messaging are off track. You are stuck.

Today, people have the attention span of a gnat. How and what you deliver are critically important. Appealing to a specific target readership is so very critical.

You too can design and create a useful Business Plan that earns the interest and attention of your intended audience. Here's how.

The most successful businessperson I ever knew would summarize his entire Business Plan into 10 PowerPoint slides, with four key, brief thoughts on each slide. It worked.

Focus is also key in any Business Plan. How do you define the most effective model? The shortest one that delivers the punch, gets the audience to react, and gets you what you have set out to achieve.

Whatever it is, package yourself to interest, attract, and capture the attention of your intended audience, be they investors, foundations, government, strategic alliance partners, or any other party that can do you good.

Knowing your target audience is of paramount important.

- What are they looking for in a Business Plan?
- What Business Plan style, content, and format do they prefer? Ask them before you create a massive manifesto document.
- What has their track record been in supporting businesses? Ask and they will proudly tell you.
- Who is on their decision-making committee, and what are their holdings and interests? Dig. Ask around. Do your homework. Aim for your Plan to appeal to them.

- Are they active players, or tire-kickers? Don't ask, but find out.
- Who have they supported in the past, and what can that party tell you about their experience? Ask, and find out.
- Who have they rejected in the past? Again, find out and ask where others went wrong.
- For investors, what are their "hot buttons"? The next Apple Computers? Whales? Money? Bio pharmacology? Money? Multifold return exit strategies? Adding value to their current portfolios? Money (think I mentioned that already)?

There is a quicksand trap inherent in Business Plans. Here it is. **It's not what you want to tell your audience, it's what they want and need to hear.** Simple, and yet I can build a Tower of Babylon with the multitude 200-, 300-, and even 500-page Business Plans I was asked to review. I doubt that I finished even one cover to cover.

In one instance, I became involved in an economic recovery effort that revolved around a rural community in trouble. It had lost its key manufacturing operation that represented over 90 percent of the community's tax base. Unemployment was destined to reach 50 percent. Even the local grocery store, bank, and bowling area were shuttering their doors (although the bowling alley, being the local cannabis dealing house, was likely the greatest economic loss of the three deserters).

The government engaged an ivory tower consulting firm (not mine) with high hopes that this savior would lead them back to economic boom. The firm sent in their team of junior plodders and delivered a 300-page report with 175 "to do now" recommendations, practically one per three town residents. It was a pretty report. Well written. Graphically appealing. Well referenced and absolutely intimidatingly useless for its intended audience. That one last factor was overlooked, hence the reference to "ivory tower."

My firm was then engaged as "the cleanup squad." We moved into the community for one month, met the public wherever they gathered for coffee, and schmoozed with the regional champions, that is, those who could undertake and spearhead change.

We delivered one recommendation; build a penitentiary. The area was quite isolated and ideal for this kind of facility. It also promised full, unionized, and pensioned employment. There was a predetermined needs assessment done and all parties came to the table. Our recommendation was gratefully accepted. In fact, it has been expanded twice over the years, a testament to the proliferation of really bad guys.

Again, the lesson is that any Business Plan, Feasibility Study, Viability Study, Risk Assessment, Economic Plan, Investor Review, and so on, you undertake must be designed to achieve an outcome. Otherwise all your efforts are headed to the quicksand pits of waste, futility, and perdition.

Workbook

1. Chose a "cause" as to why you might need to generate a Business Plan (or other plan/study) and identify exactly what you would want it to achieve.
2. Design a Table of Contents for a Business Plan you would write or support.
3. Having completed that, create a 10-slide PowerPoint with a maximum of four key, brief thoughts on each slide. No pretty pictures. No scintillating graphics. Just the "need to hit home" stuff.
4. Test it all out with a trusted associate. Never launch it without objective feedback. So, how did you make out?

Do Your Homework.
Then Do It Again.

Business decisions based on kneejerk reactions, complacency, or vision-impeding blinders can be toxic. However, worse yet, taking action hampered by a lack of (or flawed) objective, timely homework/research can be comically fatal. Not funny comical. Just the very woeful kind.

- Does anyone not own a PC? Xerox invented the first PC but never exploited the opportunity.
- Kodak did not recognize digital imaging/photography as its future. It struggled late in the game to play catch-up, but it was way outpaced.
- Blockbuster turned down the opportunity to partner with the fledgling Netflix business and stuck with its store video rental business model until it went bankrupt in 2010. Netflix, on the other hand, is now a $28 billion company.

How can you possibly make important decisions, the kind that dictate the future direction of your business, without doing your homework, then doing it again until you are certain that you have mined deeply enough? You can't.

"Do your homework" is a mantra of business. Whether it's to research markets, competition, industry trends, credit granting, measuring the impact of technology, or gaging customer satisfaction, this function is too frequently carried out with preconceived outcomes.

Too often a business's critical decisions are also based on homework assigned to an undertrained overwhelmed newbie in the company who has some extra time. Qualifications and methodology be damned. The process is often not given enough credence. Its importance is undervalued.

But, aside from decisions based on prepossessed outcomes, believing what you want to believe, and/or sketchy homework likely carried out by the lowest common denominator on your team, there are even more research problems. Being aware of these obstacles can help you avoid them. These are a few that have gotten me into trouble. Learn from my scars.

- **TOO MUCH INFORMATION**: This is where the good tidbits get buried in a mountain of information, much of which is pure rubbish/fill and has little or nothing to do with the issue at hand. Brain dump does not mean garbage dump. It's just the fluff that needs to be separated so that you can focus on the fruit of your research.
- **DATED MATERIAL**: It seems that nothing ever disappears off the Web. For the untrained eye, the more information the merrier, even though some of it is painfully out of date. Technology is especially susceptible to being leapfrogged in a flash. Be aware of anything that should have been retired to the "home" ages ago.
- **COST OF RESEARCH**: Carrying out homework costs money; joining trade organizations, buying industry reports, exploring websites and social media, and talking with people. Lots of people. Don't shortchange the process with a restrictive budget for your researcher(s).
- **UNREALISTIC TIMEFRAME**: Because you need to decide something by next week, don't expect all the homework to be completed within your short timeframe. It's not fair. You do not want to make a decision based on incomplete research that fits your timing, and little else.
- **USE OF TECHNOLOGY**: There are apps and tools to facilitate researchers. Give your people the resources to access anything they need to. In my company I always had one technologist (i.e., nerd) who kept us abreast of the latest and greatest tools.
- **RESEARCH DONE IN CHANGING TIMES**: Timing is critical, especially in economic sectors that change rapidly or where circumstances change the way we do business, for example, political unrest or pandemics. Information becomes

out-of-date quickly. Carry out your homework often to reflect uncertain and ever-changing times.

- **REASONABLE DOUBT**: It sounds like an old courtroom TV episode, but it's a critical component of research; people lie. There, I've said it. Don't believe everything you dig up. People exaggerate, embellish, or omit critical information for any number of reasons; protecting their market niche, scaring off competition, and other self-interest motives. Look for and believe the common denominators in your research, that is, the same information that comes up often through various sources. Eliminate the extremes. They could be inaccurate and misleading. Even malicious.

In one of my playful moods, I tested this theory by responding creatively to a credit company calling for a background on my firm. By the time I was done reporting, I hardly recognized my inflated company. Two weeks later I asked a colleague to pull a report on us. Everything I had told them was taken at face value and regurgitated into this report. I was proud to be credited with 1,650 employees with offices around the globe. If only…. But I did contact the agency to correct the data. That only took four months.

Workbook

1. Select an opportunity you had been considering.
2. Assign the homework to three people in your organization, one relatively new, and two more experienced in research.
3. Define the parameters of what you want explored and suggest a reasonable timeframe to complete the task.
4. However, give one of the experienced researchers only half the time and half the budget to complete their task.
5. Their deliverable should be comprised of the research findings and recommendations for the company.
6. Compare the results. Now you likely understand the fundamentals of this chapter.

You Always Need Money

I have never come across a stuck enterprise that didn't need some new money. It's one of those universal laws; the sun rises in the east and you always need more money.

By now you have probably used up your own financial reserves and burnt some bridges with your friends and family who may have previously invested in your venture. But now even your Mother won't return your calls. Time for a new playbook. You need to step back, reset, and develop a solid plan "B."

The place to start is a somewhat brutal review of what has transpired to get you here. It's not all bad. You have likely made some progress, learned a lot, and achieved some minor successes. Now is the time to repackage your knowledge and experiences, both the good and the bad, as product research and development.

Most successful endeavors have overcome numerous early failures. It's an inevitable part of the growth curve. Nobody gets through the entrepreneurial experience unscathed.

I was once involved with a company that had amassed a truly impressive string of failures. We were pioneering a new product for a market that was just being born. There was no existing road map for the most basic parameters like "what should this product look like?" or "how would customers use our product?" and "where would they buy it?" A lot of unknowns.

We launched several versions of our product and each one failed to catch on. We were certain that each successive version was the solution. It wasn't. Eventually, we stumbled upon the winning formula and then packaged all our failures as market research and product development.

We then portrayed our company as the leading industry expert in our new product category. This was a classic case of putting lipstick on a pig but it turned out to be a big positive for our new investors as they saw value in our extensive "research," which we took to be our earlier failures. It worked.

When rejigging your own company for new money, here are a couple of issues to focus on:

The Problem: Acknowledge that there is a problem and prepare for some pain.

The Goals: Clarify your goals both short term and long term.

The Numbers: Review all your sales, budget, and financial numbers.

The Revenue Model: Restate how your company will make money.

The Plan: Polish your revised Business Plan and ensure that all the pieces add up to one compelling story.

Now that you have figured out how to structure your breakout, you will probably be faced with the ugly truth that you don't have the money necessary to implement it. After you have tipped the couch over in search of nickels and dimes, the most common first step may be returning to your friends, family, and the initial investors that supported you. This is often a hard sell as they already financed your venture and may not be keen on additional investing.

This is a gentle way of warning you. Expect some slammed doors. You are best to seek a new group of "friends" with your reworked plan.

Your next stop may be your (un)friendly bank. This is usually a short meeting. Sadly, the banking community does not support stalled or rejigged ventures unless you have a stable cash flow and a healthy balance sheet. The best that you can usually do via traditional banking is a personal loan backed by your own assets, usually your house or other hard assets. Not a very appealing option.

Alternative financing opportunities are out there.

Community Development Finance Institutions: There are many of these throughout the country that are community-based, nonprofit lenders that target small businesses with loans. They are generally regarded as less rigid than banks and more focused on local employment.

Partnerships: Gaining a strategic partner can bring needed capital to a business in the form of an equity investment rather than a traditional loan. Loans can be paid off, retired, and then they are gone, but partners, not so much. Proceed with caution.

Angels: Angel investors are always a good idea. Even if your venture is currently too early for them, they will keep an eye on your progress and may be part of your future. Generally, angels are more supportive of you and your business than venture capitalists who are solely intent on reducing their risks and increasing their returns.

Family Offices: These are usually investment vehicles that manage their family wealth and often include a family member that scouts for investment opportunities. Like angels, they vary vastly on their investment parameters, but it's always worth knocking on their door.

Crowdfunding: I'm a big fan of crowdfunding for young and rejigged companies. It's easy, fast, and effective. Crowdfunding is raising billions of dollars every year and continues to grow in popularity with investors. There are many different platforms available. Find the one that is targeted to your type of venture.

Peer-to-Peer Lending (P2P): "P2P" lending is another creation of the Internet. It has been called a hybrid of crowdfunding because it connects private lenders with deserving borrowers. Unlike crowdfunding, these transactions are actual loans.

So, don't just concentrate on one financing avenue. There is usually more than one option for you. Work them all.

Workbook

1. State your business goal in 20 words, maximum.
2. Define your unit economic/business model.
   - Calculate revenue, cost, expenses, and Gross Margin per unit
3. List your potential new money sources.
4. Research to find out what makes each money source tick, that is, what are their investment interests and priorities.
5. How much new money do you really need? Start small.

An NDA Is Not Your Savior. There's Much Better Protection.

Paranoia in business tends to run deep. The consensus is that someone will steal your idea, claim it as their own, and celebrate their success on the company's new mega yacht named after your venture, say, "Disco Revival." You may not be that paranoid, actually.

Enter the lawyers, and the Non-Disclosure Agreement (NDA); the overpriced, mostly boilerplate document designed to protect the interests of all parties entering into a confidential relationship. Does it?

In principal, an NDA sounds stellar. However, human nature and goodwill are often displaced by old-fashioned greed. Before you leap lemming-like into the NDA quicksand, think of the downstream scenario and who you might be dealing with once the glitter is faded.

Show me any NDA and I will show you a handful of escape clauses. The NDA often purports to have "teeth," but in truth, most NDAs have wobbly dentures at best.

- Define "confidential." It's not easy. It is often set out in general terms, or overbroad, with far too generic descriptives that are easy to work around.
- Confidentiality applies only if you are the sole signatory to the NDA. Otherwise, any confidential material that gets out can have come from any number of sources.
- Often there is an inequality between NDA signatories. In the case of a dispute, the wealthier, more powerful signatory and their potent legal counsel have a distinct advantage. Understand your punching power.

Most of the NDAs I have issued and signed have been reasonably simple documents without pages full of "whereas and heretofores." However, the first time I got burned was when I got into bed with a cheat.

I dreamt of all those dollar bills of investment coming my way instead of paying attention to the niggling feeling of imminent danger tapping me incessantly on my shoulder. I leapt and lost. My investor took my idea to the market and became even richer, at my expense.

I eventually lost track of him, but was delighted to hear that he fleeced someone higher up in the food chain, and is probably now playing canasta with Jimmy Hoffa.

A signed NDA is only as good as the signers' willingness to honor it. That is sometimes a stretch, but there are strategies that can protect your interests when reaching out to investors, partners, funders, and other parties important to safeguarding your business.

1. Go with your gut feel. It has gotten you to where you are today. The proviso here is that greed and shades of desperation can push the boundaries of your survival instinct. Don't let it.

2. There is always one piece of the opportunity puzzle that is critical for your project or business. It could be the intellectual property, the chemical composition of product "X," or a step in the production process. Whatever it is, leave it out of your information sharing until you are extremely comfortable with the other parties.

3. Don't deal with crooks. I think my mother tried to teach me that. But we cannot survive in business by always peering over our shoulder. So, do background checks on your "targets," their experience and history in dealing with others, and their reputation in the marketplace. With today's resources, very little can stay hidden for long. Thank you, Google.

4. Work with friends and business associates who can provide you with a warm, fuzzy introduction to whomever you want to work with. This generally creates a bond far stronger than an NDA.

5. Our excitement about business opportunities often leads us to talk too much. Keep your ego in check. Speak cautiously and only when it is to your advantage to do so.

6. Use your own NDA and your own lawyer, not one drafted by the other party. You are the one who needs to be protected.

7. Think carefully as to why you are approaching the other party. Define what you want out of the relationship and what you are prepared to give up. Perhaps the answer is to start small, on your own, foregoing the need to second-guess that NDA in front of you.

Sharing information is always a delicate balancing act between the excitement of going after someone or something you can almost reach out and touch versus holding your cards too closely and getting rejected. It's a matter of harmony.

My client had developed an advanced process for raising various seafood species in a landlocked environment. It was a highly technical process that encompassed a number of proprietary "green" technologies.

There was an interested licensee, but a background check on their company yielded a few question marks about past involvements. In this case, I considered that an NDA had little value.

The licensee was leery to pay until the entire safeguard of the process had been revealed. It was a game of trust-mistrust.

Instead, I drafted a "pay as you play" agreement. That is, we negotiated a price for the license. Then, we had the licensee pay hefty, nonrefundable installments as my client revealed tidbits of his process and technology. The payout was complete at the same time as my client revealed the last piece of the process puzzle.

Workbook

1. Research NDA templates that are available, or ask your lawyer to provide you with blank boilerplates.

2. Draft three NDAs ranging from a simple two-pager to a sphincter-tightening legalese manifesto with loads of restrictions and potential penalties.

3. Ask several business associates which they would be comfortable signing. This will allow you to know how far you can push others. There's no sense in creating an NDA that others are leery to sign, so find the happy medium.

Go Extrovert Yourself

Do you enjoy being the public face and flavor of your business? Enjoy socializing and schmoozing? Being an admired role model and inspiring leader for your team? Devour all the attention that fuels your extroversion?

Yes? Great!

No? Then you are likely stuck in a performance void. You need to climb out of the quicksand before you sink into the oblivion inhabited by business wallflowers. Don't be an observer or bystander. Be a player.

Think of this as an influential business tool that can generate far-reaching results for your company. And for those who do not have the natural pizzazz to pull this off, rest assured that it is a learnable skill. With some practice and training, you too can escape the shadow of business persona mediocrity and bound into the limelight.

There are a number of features that best define the business extrovert. Consider this a "shopping list," but you do not need to fill your cart with ALL of these to be characterized as an extrovert.

1. **PERSONALITY:** Outgoing, effusively enthusiastic, and demonstrative. Extroverts also tend to be those "touchy feely" people at get-togethers who reach out physically to connect. Embracing others defines importance to the relationship, whether it be genuine or contrived.
2. **DRESS:** The most outwardly visible element of the extrovert. Let's say distinctive and different as opposed to flashy and clown-like. Stylish. Colorful. Often "talk about" worthy. It is a uniform.
3. **PRESENCE:** Everywhere, and at every opportunity; social media, events, written, or broadcast media. This is the kind of repetitive in-your-face activity that cultivates your recognition and awareness in the marketplace. It's like Pavlov's dogs' conditioning; others see you, hear you, read about you, and they instantly get to know you (maybe even salivate in the process, kind of like Milkah, one of Ivan Pavlov's favorite test animals).

4. **PARTICIPATION**: Extroverts are joiners; organizations (fraternal as well as industry); volunteers for worthwhile (and high exposure) causes; guest speakers and columnists and, wherever possible, sought out for providing expert sound bites in media reporting.

5. **REBELLIOUS**: This feature has a wide range of delivery, from shameful attention-grabbers to charming. The former tend to be "flash-in the-pan" types. The latter are embraced. So, be edgy but embraceable.

6. **CONTRARION**: Alternate positions and opinions tend to get noticed. The extrovert offers up different points of view with just enough "what did they say?" contrary to established viewpoints. They do that without becoming insufferable.

7. **RISK**: Risk is personal. Everyone has their own levels of acceptable risk. However, extroverts tend to push the envelope, or at least appear to do so, but often in a well-calculated fashion. The end result is that they get noticed and admired, and those are the prevalent goals in their exercise.

8. **HERO**: Extroverts are often cited as business heroes, those leading the charge. That could range from instigating changes in an industry, to spearheading a funding drive for a worthwhile cause. Regardless, the extrovert is the character that leads the masses and does not get buried in the swelling multitude following behind them.

9. **TAKING A STAND**: Often described as stubborn or intractable, the extrovert does not generally waver from an opinion or action. Sometimes the "courage of their conviction" backfires if there is an outcry. Some degree of flexibility is necessary to bend slightly to the whims of others. That minimal/modest submission actually increases peoples' respect for the extrovert.

Respect, attention, relating well to others, perceived as competent—these are all features associated with extroverts, and the kind of strengths that can readily steer conversations and seek out rewards, namely, connections, opportunities, and business. They have street value.

There are a number of cons as well, namely, extroverts tend to believe (and act upon) their own hype, are often power hungry, skim over decisions deemed of lesser importance (but aren't), and carry an attitude of disdain. The negative side of the extrovert personality cannot be overlooked.

There is, however, a halfway measure, and that is people cast by circumstance into the extrovert domain. Classic introverts such as Bill Gates, Steve Wozniak, and Warren Buffett, whom we assume are extroverts, are not. Their public performances speak to their shyness and discomfort in being in the spotlight. They are creative, innovative introverts. This halfway measure of being "somewhat perceived as an extrovert" may be a feature you may wish to adopt and nurture.

Workbook

1. Create a two-column chart that you will use to identify your extrovert features (left column) and introvert characteristics (right column).
   - Anything you would like to change?
   - How would you do that?
   - Why would you do that (how will it impact your business)?
2. Identify three extrovert business personalities you know.
   - Is there anything they do that you might want to adopt into your own repertoire?
   - What would that do for you, business-wise?

Business Is Kind of Like Theatre But With Bigger Props

There's an old joke about a businessman who isn't all that impressive to his colleagues or clients. It goes, "Whenever he enters a room, it feels like somebody left."

If you are seeking business-to-business clients or prospects or even distributors/buyers, you will often have to impress and win these people over to become clients. You have to have presence when you enter any business gathering. You also have to portray yourself as this confident leader to your own people: your partners, employees, suppliers, and investors.

Actors call it "stage presence." Politicians call it charisma. The unequipped entrepreneur, however, is heading to the quicksand pit of invisibility.

Have you ever analyzed or evaluated your "presence"? Or asked someone close to you to do it with you? The impression you make when you enter a room, whether it's a boardroom, an office, a function room, an auditorium, wherever, you need to be projecting confidence. Total confidence. Even if you don't feel it 100 percent.

For you to appeal to your potential clients, they need to see you as their "hero." You are there to solve their problems, not yours. We've all met those women and men who make you feel like "yes, you are exactly what I need." It is not magic; you can learn how to give off those vibes.

Think of yourself as an actor preparing to go on stage or in front of the cameras. Because that is precisely what you are doing. So, you should approach it in the same way.

An "Actor" Prepares

Know your character. You are "playing" the accomplished head of your company who is there to make your clients more successful. You are confident, charming, friendly, helpful, and attentive.

Know what you're going to say. I don't mean memorizing lines—that can make you sound stiff and ill-prepared. But know what it is you can do for your prospects. Know their business as well as you know your own so you can talk about it intelligently off the top of your head. Actors do their homework; you need to do yours. Actors also rehearse, and yes, you should too.

Stay focused. It's very easy to get distracted in group settings with lots of people wandering in and out of the conversation. Focus on listening and solving their needs. Remember to catch, not pitch.

Wardrobe. Think of this as your "costume." Make sure it's right. Notice I said "right," not fancy. If your business is operating guided fishing tours through the north woods, don't dress in a three-piece pinstripe suit and power tie (unless of course, you are at a formal event). Conversely, if you are providing financial/wealth management advice, don't look like you just stepped off an Alaskan crab boat. Match your wardrobe to your client's perceptions and expectations.

Personal Grooming. Is your target audience largely hipster millennials? Don't look like you're five years behind the times in terms of hairstyle, facial hair, piercings, or tattoos. Again, be aware of grooming and style trends of your target market. Are they conservative? If so, maybe do not wear "extreme" or preppy clothing. If they are more easy-going or even a little out there themselves, you have more leeway.

An important note on tattoos: If your tattoos, or jewelry, piercings, and so on, are cultural, then display them with pride. Likewise, if they are integral to your business. If, however, they are personal grooming choices, then be aware of what they might imply to your prospects and, if necessary, balance the look so you can still be yourself without scaring small children.

When you have all these guidelines firmly in your head, then practice your conversations in the mirror, with friends, family, colleagues, whoever will listen. Be ready to answer any question. If there is a question you can't answer, do NOT try to lie or tap dance your way around it. Simply say that you don't have that information at the moment but will get it to you as soon as possible. Then do it. It's yet another opportunity to touch base with a prospect.

If you do all of these things, you will be perceived as the expert in your field. If you're not quite there, fake it until you are and work your tail off to get there.

Workbook

Try this at a function like a networking session and have fun.

Choose your persona. Who do you want to be?
- Decide how you want to be perceived.

Choose your costume (attire):
- Attire is a "costume."
- Wear the right costume: formal, casual, cultural, and so on.

Making an entrance:
- Enter the room and don't slink.
- Take a moment to scope your potential contacts.
- Spot one person to go to and strike up a conversation.

After the entrance:
- Make and maintain eye contact.
- Be aware of the power of proximity, but don't invade others' personal space.
- Listen to what your prospects are saying, then offer your feedback, not prepared platitudes.
- Ask questions. People are rarely too busy to talk about themselves.

Most importantly: Enjoy the performance. It can be exhilarating.

Social Moodia Versus Social Media

Social Moodia

Social media marketeers tell us that over half the world's population are active social media users. That represents over four billion people. You've just got to rush in, right? Pretty impressive numbers, but a lot of that activity sounds like this: "I love that you share my fondness for canary yellow accessories" or "I am sad that my dinner out with friends at Paesano Pasta was a total bore. OMG."

That's social "moodia," and it's a pretty prevalent part of the social media environment.

From a business perspective, social moodia is noisy, crowded, and virtually impossible to control or direct. It is vast and directionless, even with influencers' millions (real, fake, purchased user databases, or bot-generated) of followers. It's a place to get lost and stuck. Anonymity is never far away.

Celebrity influencers aside (who could not lust after the Kardashians?); most no-name influencers have seen their follower numbers shrink dramatically and their marketplace impact diminished. It's a case of cyclical popularity. The two widespread clichés "being famous on Instagram is the same as being rich on Monopoly" and "you can't pay the bills with likes" exemplifies the dangers of relying heavily on social moodia.

Stuck entrepreneurs tend to wrap themselves around the magic of numbers of social media users and forget the one true doctrine of marketing; while social moodia can help proliferate your brand, assuming you focus down to target audiences and markets, this activity does not ring up sales or drive conversions to your company's customer base. Those are huge issues.

Yet small businesses are generally big believers and users of social moodia, with heightened expectations, and at the expense of not carrying out other more effective market strategies where results can be measured. That's just delusional.

Social Media

Social media (as opposed to "moodia"), however, is an exceptional tool that can help humanize your company, and help you engage, stay in touch with, and expand your customer base. It should be a tool to drive traffic to your own website, and not a stand-alone strategy.

Some of these social media platforms include Facebook, LinkedIn, Twitter, YouTube, Pinterest, Instagram, Shopify, WhatsApp, Snapchat, Flickr, WordPress, Blogger, Wikipedia, or Reddit, and professed user numbers range from several hundred million to billions. The freebie days are mostly gone, though. The leading platforms have monetized their business model and that means if you want to consider anything beyond fluff pieces and marginal exposure, it will cost you.

Regardless, you cannot still wander aimlessly. You need to clearly identify why you are getting involved, how each platform can benefit you depending on its reach, how it fits into your overall content marketing strategy, and how it can meet your expectations that can include any of the following:

- Increases awareness of your products or services.
- Increases traffic to your website.
- Enhances brand recognition.
- New customer attraction.
- Sales lead generation.
- Supports timely dissemination of information about you.
- Simple and cost-effective way to tell your story.
- Allows you to engage, interact, and stay connected with your customer base.
- Enables you to monitor what is being said about you.
- Provides early warning of potential issues that may impact your business.

All of these sound great, but most outcomes are notoriously difficult or impossible to accurately track. The best you can hope for are qualitative results that enhance the effectiveness of a broader content marketing strategy.

There are other pitfalls and shortcomings you need to be keenly aware of.

- You don't own your content. You are sharing it and the platform itself can redistribute it for financial gain. Ever see your material crop up elsewhere under another company's banner? I have. It's pretty disconcerting, so keep your "secret sauce" close to you.
- Ninety percent (90 percent) of online searches start with a well-established search engine such as Google, or its direct competitors. Social media will account a fraction (3 percent) of enticing visitors to your website.
- Social media is hackable, and containing the backlash can be painful once the fire spreads.
- Social media marketeers or influencers will quote big numbers to get you as a client. Ask them to prove their pitch.
- Published content (i.e., blogs) can generate results, but only downstream. There is little instant gratification, regardless of what pitch you are told.

  I once wrote a regular blog for an online entrepreneurial training company called "The No BS School of Business." The blogs were supposed to be part of a full content marketing approach, which never happened. Instead, the owner put my blogs out there where they got lost among millions of others (six hundred million blogs as of 2021). He waited for the signups to roll in, and I am still waiting for my royalty check. It's only been four years, so maybe anytime soon.

The bottom line is to use social media wisely, integrated with more diverse content marketing, and steer everything to your website which is where sales can be generated and competitors' clients can be offered a better alternative, namely, you.

And as far as social moodia goes, don't get stuck. Consider it as entertainment at best.

Workbook

1. List your top five marketing vehicles that you use for your business, including social media.
   (a) How do you know for sure they are working?
   (b) How much of your budget do you commit to each area?
   (c) What is the cost per lead that's cost per $1 revenue generated?
2. Ask customers where they heard about you?
3. When they think about you, what medium do they connect with your company?
4. Track their responses.

Befriend the Resolute Gatekeeper

Having difficulties getting in to see that sales prospect? Interlopers be warned. I am the gatekeeper, the unflinching sentry guard who prevents unwanted traffic from filtering past me to whomever you are desperate to reach. My job is to keep my boss on track, away from distraction. You are such a distraction.

Don't underestimate the power and effectiveness of these sentinels. An encounter with a gatekeeper in the course of business effectively screening calls, visitors, and electronic messages, can be a daunting roadblock; especially if they sense that the motive behind your call may likely represent an annoyance to their employer. And the good defenders possess a seventh sense. Play it wrong, and you become a mildly irritating footnote.

All is not lost. There are a series of strategies that can help you win the attention and affection of the gatekeeper, or to skillfully circumvent them entirely; mostly by being "human" in your approach and attitude. It is a process of establishing trust. But before we get to the good morsels of advice, let's see if you recognize any of the reasons (below) as to how you may likely be messing up, and not even realizing it.

1. Deflection is what gatekeepers do. It is generally one of their primary tasks. Chances are they are smarter at keeping you out than you are at getting in. Never underestimate the gatekeeper. This is NOT a level-playing field. Do you overestimate your ability to woo?

2. Gatekeepers seem to develop a sixth sense for those who lie, bullshit, or try to deceive their way in. They are equipped with sensors fine-tuned to recognize when they are being snowed. Did you ever get bounced for playing the arrogant hotshot? The aggrieved party? The charmer? The "pity-me" needy one?

3. These sentries take great pride in their roles. Don't trivialize their power with any semblance of condescension or sickeningly-sweet, superficial flattery. Regard them as equals.

- I had a senior sales rep whose reputation as a charmer far exceeded his ability to close sales. Something was wrong. I decided to accompany him on a sales call. His tactic to get past the gatekeeper was launching into a clip from a cheesy bar pick-up scene. He was seducing the gatekeeper, sitting on the edge of her desk, and launching shallowly camouflaged innuendos. Everyone, other than him, was revolted. He was in mid-performance when we were rejected by the gatekeeper.
- My comment to him when we walked out was, "It's no wonder your sales are slumping, Casanova. I'm surprised we are not being sued. Don't bother coming back to the office. We will ship your personal belongings and severance pay to your home."

Having now covered the "don'ts," the ones that get you into trouble, let us launch into some strategies that can work for you in traversing the no-mans-land.

1. The best circumnavigation is to be referred by a mutual business friend or multiplier. This will translate to instant trust and positive communication with the gatekeeper.
2. Develop an abbreviated rapid-fire elevator pitch that the guardian can quickly wrap their arms around and gage if you can be of benefit to their senior and should be allowed through.
3. Don't schmooze. Everyone is too busy for small talk. Get to the point, with the most important feature being their recognizing what's in it for them. What quantifiable benefits can result from your interaction with their superior? That is a key "hot button."
4. They may be friendly to deal with, but don't assume they are your friend. It is most likely their coping strategy, one that may give you a false sense of having made progress in piercing their protective

armor. Work to build a relationship on a professional, mutually respectful basis.

5. Don't use e-mail or social media or messaging to get past the gatekeeper. It rarely works, especially in our obscenely crowded electronic environment. Whatever doesn't end up in spam is easily dismissed with a "no" reply. "No." See how easy that was?

6. The one exception here is the Executive Assistant (EA) gatekeeper who acts as an extension to the decision maker. So be very aware of the level of gatekeeper you are dealing with.

   The best EA I ever knew was Elizabeth, my own EA. She understood my habits, my priorities, my pet projects, and my need to focus. Watching her work was an art form. I actually learned from her unflinching style and her allegiance to me. And it was blissfully entertaining.

   Stay on track without meandering away to other shiny tidbits.

7. These sentries have a common checklist of "good versus bad" that you will be judged by, and whether you will be granted safe passage to their bosses. Understand what drives them, and address their issues.

8. Do your premeeting/visit research. Learn about the company. Having that knowledge helps create a common bond between you both.

Dealing successfully with the EA—sentinel—guard—go-between—watchperson—sentry—gatekeeper is an important skillset. Work on your approach. Practice. Learn from when you succeed, and also from when you get rebuffed.

I often asked, on my way out of meetings, what persuaded the gatekeeper to let me enter the inner sanctum. If I was rejected, I inquired why. That's how we learn. Ask.

Workbook

1. List five actions and opening gambits you generally employ to deal with gatekeepers.

2. Find a business associate who has an effective gatekeeper you can "borrow."

3. Try your approaches with them in a role-playing exercise.

4. For any of the approaches that seem to create a smidgen of recognition or interest on their part, pursue that direction until you are able to refine your strategy.

5. Create four lists: What worked? What didn't work? What do you need to incorporate into your own strategies? What do you need to discard?

Is Your Integrity for Rent? Maybe No. Maybe Yes

You've been in business for a while, and it's tougher than you imagined. You're putting in the 12- to 18-hour days. You forget how many kids you have. You have trouble remembering your spouse's name. Sales are sluggish, the client funnel is far from full, expenses are rising, and revenues are down.

This is quite possibly the most important point in your journey. You ask yourself, "What am I willing to do to get unstuck? To save my business?"

Let's present both sides of the equation. Then you decide.

Making the Case for Integrity NOT for Sale

It's so tempting to take on a dodgy project, or even a questionable client. Or worse, be less than above board with your existing clients, making big promises you know will be hard if not impossible to keep.

Maybe it's padding your bill a little. Or "prebilling" to pay off suppliers. I'll "borrow" from the media budget, or the production budget, or …"It will just be this once until I get back on my feet." It is very, very easy for "just this once" to become "just one more time."

Selling your integrity can be seen as nothing more than a lease-to-own. Here are a couple of things you need to determine:

1. What barriers are you willing to ignore and which ones will you hold firm on?
2. Base your decision on whether any "lapse" will irreparably damage your integrity.

There are some hard and fast rules that you should NEVER break:

1. Do not put your client in jeopardy, even for one second.
2. Don't hide important things from your client (e.g., you are going to miss your shipping date which will have a seriously detrimental effect on your client's business). If you get a reputation for having a loose relationship with truth and honesty, you will get into trouble. Maybe not right away, but it will happen. Clients talk among themselves.

My company was asked to bid on a large economic study for a major city. Big ticket. Lots of prestige and fees for the winning bid. When I read who the "Request for Bids" was issued by, I immediately discarded the notion of bidding.

You see, the bidding agent had developed a nasty habit of issuing Requests for Proposals (RFPs) and then awarding the contracts to his pet suppliers. Always the same one or two groups. The RFPs were just his way of having competitive bids on hand if he ever got audited, which he eventually did when enough of us underdogs complained.

Since nobody in government ever gets fired, he was simply demoted to a position where his toughest decision was ordering HB or 2H pencils. And his pet suppliers were blackballed and never saw contract daylight again.

Now, I realize that business is rarely black and white, but the more shades of gray you see, the easier it is for your integrity to become available for rent, if not outright purchase.

Making the Case for Integrity FOR Sale

I must admit that, personally, I am a proponent for renting your integrity but not selling it. The latter reeks of permanence, which is a fatal situation. Think of every gangster/mafia movie you have ever watched, and witnessed the weak being bullied or put in harms-way by the villain. Business is no different.

There is a cardinal rule that is my mantra; do whatever it takes, within legal and (predominantly) moral limits, to survive and win in business.

That denotes being flexible and elastic in your ethics, which translates to renting out your integrity when the need or opportunity arises. The key word here is "need," as in what you require to weather a storm, or "opportunity" that represents a necessary win for your company.

Would you put in a bid having some advance knowledge of the host's undisclosed preferences? I would, in a heartbeat. That is, unless I became aware of those "preferences" through nefarious means. Elasticity only stretches so far.

It is said that integrity enhances your reputation and attracts and retains customers. While that is possibly true, I have always found that the marketplace playing field is sufficiently large and diverse enough that there are always enough players to fill your order book.

I am not condoning discarding your integrity. Far from it. I am advocating to keep an open mind and focus on the most important factor; your very survival. And winning, of course.

Your integrity is an asset. How you choose to protect it or cash it in will be based on circumstance. Both scenarios have lasting after-effects on who you are and how you are perceived in the business community. Think of that before you act.

I have had my share of odd clients. In hindsight, I stuck it out with them by renting, but not foregoing my integrity.

- The born-again religious believer who led us all in lengthy prayers before every management meeting. Even though I was, and still am a devout agnostic, I joined in. It was the least I could do to stay in his good grace (pun intended).
- The major dairy production executive who insisted we all sample his ripe, "designer" cheeses at each get-together. My dairy allergy sickened me, but I soldiered on.
- The miscreant who owned a plant to produce dog treats made out of rawhide (bull penises, actually) and insisted we all listen to his problems about his supply chain. I once asked him how the bulls felt about him, and if his photo was on "Wanted" posters in bullpens everywhere. My joke was not appreciated, but I couldn't help myself.

Workbook

1. Think of three situations where the temptation to shade your integrity could raise its head.
   - How could you be compromised, and how can you avoid being compromised?
2. Think of three situations where you did, to a degree, compromise your integrity.
   - Did the benefits outweigh the risks?
3. Think of three situations in your business dealings where you might be justified to bend the integrity rules without major repercussions.
   - Would you? Why or why not?

Marketing Ethics
Are Also Elastic

Don't get stuck in the world of dull and mundane advertising and promotion. Do what works for you, not what moral principles the "industry" and its self-serving guardians may set forth.

Building your brand and public awareness is not achieved by, say, an ecstatic, coiffed, and alluring stereotypical housewife dancing around the kitchen embracing a spacey-looking mop. Oh wait, I'm running out to buy one right now!

Is that supposed to be in good taste? Doubtful. But who is to judge?

Marketing ethics is an ideal; a gray area guide designed and advocated by advertising organizations and associations who, themselves, bend and often fracture the rules of "right and wrong," "good taste and bad." Any industry that professes to regulate itself answers to no one. In other words, it is a whitewashing public relations exercise. Don't fall into the trap.

Whatever is your content marketing strategy, you will undoubtedly build a fan base with some groups and, in our world of hypersensitivity, you will certainly alienate others. The trick is to hit the right buttons with your intended target audience, regardless of how crass you may be perceived by those you don't give a damn about. Be brave.

Sweet Jesus, an ice cream chain, incites people with products such as Red Rapture and Hella Hazelnut, and claims just tasting their ice cream is a religious experience. Their uber-trendy target market is the young, counter-culture crowd. Apparently, few church goers here. And yet they are successful, as outrageous as they are. They know their audience.

On the other hand, some companies play it safe by walking both sides of the marketing street. Dove Soap ran simultaneous campaigns, one featuring very, very young women claiming they needed Dove to keep their skin supermodel "young" (seriously?), and another with older women seeking a touch of long-forgotten youth. Was this ethical? Not really.

In an industry that seems to have a handful of "please don't do this" guidelines, there are some things that are universally taboo. Other than these, it would seem that anything goes.

- Exaggeration—the use of turnoff superlatives such as the best, fastest, and greatest.
- Claims without substance such as "this will cure your libido," all with no proof supplied.
- Stereotypes, especially women in yesteryear-roles, or any clownish behavior by minority groups.
- Comparisons with other products. Building a reputation on others' backs is often viewed negatively.
- Exploiting defenseless groups such as children and the poor and disadvantaged. Charities walk a fine line, instilling just enough guilt to get you to respond.

The psychology of appealing to consumers and the public at large is contingent upon the mindset and the needs of the target markets. Every sector has different "hot buttons." Organic food buyers are not swayed by the same factors as those people seeking insurance, and so on. The psychological attributes of marketing as applicable to a number of key economic sectors, and content marketing examples, from consumer products to technology, can be found at www.marketing-schools.org/consumer-psychology/.

There is very little that pushes the boundaries of marketing ethics as does "guerilla marketing." It employs surprise, risk, and unconventional tactics. From Oreo cookies painted over manhole covers to Mini Coopers displayed in giant gumball machines, guerilla marketing creates messages that often go viral because they are unique and fun. However, sometimes even these go too far, or do they?

Hell Baby, the 2013 cult film, designed a promotional campaign with unattended, automated strollers rolling along the sidewalks of major cities in the United States. When stopped by concerned passers-by, a ghoulish mechanical baby figure would pop up, scream, and vomit. One of the most daring, distasteful, and successful campaigns ever. You be the judge about its ethical value. It actually generated millions of dollars worth of exposure on major networks.

The point is, in this crowded media marketplace, you need to do more to get noticed. And if it demands some marketing ethical elasticity, do it anyways.

Workbook

1. Firstly, take a serious look at your marketing and promotion efforts. Are they working? How do you know?
2. Conduct a survey of your customers, using any one of the tools available today (Google Forms, SurveryMonkey, Typeform, or others). Inquire about what your customers like about your marketing, promotions, brand, and so on. What initially attracted them to you?
3. Analyze the results. What are you being told?
4. Design a test marketing campaign that pushes the boundaries a bit without being brusque enough to alienate anyone. Remember, this is only a test.
5. Revisit your customers with another survey to gage their reaction to your more edgy campaign. Is it working? Are you on the right track? Perhaps offers coupons or gifts to those who respond.
6. Integrate the results into your content marketing strategy.

Brands Flourish, Commodities Flounder

Nothing will kill your business faster than treating your products or services as commodities.

We live in a consumer-mad age and people are overwhelmed by choice and by marketing gibberish and lies. It is unbelievably difficult to break through its commoditized categories. Without branding, it is simply impossible.

Is this where your enterprise is now? Unbranded? Commoditized? If you have let your company go this way, then you need to reverse it and change your brands to get out of the quicksand.

You likely know this, but it's worth repeating. A commodity is a product or service that is generic, like house brands or those that you find in a dollar store. They are parity products and have no branding. You have to compete on price alone, not value. And your competition, especially if they have been in the market for a while, can bury you on price. Don't go there. It's a trap.

You can enter the market that is not dominated by an established brand and get lost in a sea of "me toos." Here's an example that should put the fear of the gods of retail into you: Amazon, at the time of this writing, has 153 pages of bath bar soaps. That's just bar soap. It doesn't count liquid soaps, facial soaps, and specialty soaps. 153 pages with approximately 63 products per page!

Now, if you have just invented a revolutionary soap, without any depth to your branding, you would have a hell of a time getting noticed. And it's true across the board.

And services can be commoditized as well. A perfunctory online search for accountants in the city I live near—just one medium-sized city—has 259 listings. So, how are you going to stand out? If you are thinking to yourself, we'll be the "most professional," ask yourself how that would work. "We know numbers!" and similar empty brags won't do it. Knowing numbers, the tax code, and all the formulae is table stakes. You need a brand. Maybe it's based on exemplary service, that is, providing it, not just promising it. But without a brand, you're just another "Yeah, like we know addition and subtraction and stuff...."

The next route to commodity-ville is starting out as a game changer, may be being the first on the market with a product or service, then not doing anything to protect the brand.

Two well-known brands that suffered this fate are Band-Aid and Kleenex. Band-Aid was the first, and for a long time, the only disposable plastic/cloth bandage for small everyday nicks, cuts, scrapes, and burns. Kleenex, similarly, was the only disposable tissue of its type.

For many years, they were the only ones in their categories. Then someone else made paper tissues and marketed them under their own name. But many consumers still call all plastic bandages Band-Aids and all tissues Kleenex.

Band-Aid and Kleenex said nothing and did nothing to protect their proprietary names. The competition was happy to be thrown into the same category with these leading brands; freebie coattail marketing.

Eventually both companies decided to start marketing with phrases like "Band-Aid Brand" and "Kleenex Brand." They had to put the word "Brand" in their advertising to reclaim their once unique brand name.

Yet another path to brand loss is not understanding your own core; your own brand.

Who was the number one brand in personal listening devices in the 1980s and 1990s? Right, Sony Walkman, and no one could touch them. Until Apple created the iPod, which was truly revolutionary. Sony did not look at new technology and ask if they could develop a product that was the natural brand progression of personalized music devices. When was the last time you saw a Walkman or a Discman except at garage sales?

A more recent example of not understanding the difference between brand and product is Skype. Remember when we used Skype to talk to clients, colleagues, friends, and others through video calling? Skype likely assumed that they were 'it' and did not need to try to appeal to the marketplace. Brand? Who needs it!

Then Covid hit and all of a sudden, all meetings were carried out via the Internet, but the provider was not the logical extension of a strong existing brand. Nope. Bye-bye Skype, hello Zoom. Zoom now owns the category with Google Meet and others playing catch-up. Guess who isn't catching up? Right. Skype. It is so bad that Saturday Night Live did a sketch about a boardroom meeting at Skype's head office where the top people are shown to be comically bewildered and flustered.

There are companies who have understood their brand and allowed their consumers to exalt it. Some of the most trusted brands are still as strong as ever, and TRUST is the beating heart of a good brand. Here are just a few:

- Rolls Royce
- Lego
- Rolex
- Disney
- Nike

Worksheet

Closely examine your product or service.

1. Is your product a commodity? Is price the only way you are trying to gain entry?
2. Could your product become a commodity without your wanting it to? Remember when telephone companies were monopolies? Then new players came along and now all landline phones are sold solely on price. The telcos did not see it coming. What about your business category? Could it happen to you?
3. If your product could be commoditized, what can you do to stay relevant? Hint, it has to do with branding.
4. Are you going up against established brands? What can you do to gain a competitive advantage? How could you shape your brand?
5. Can you overcome the fear of getting a little crazy? Try it. The odd-person-out gets noticed.
6. How will you keep your brand relevant for years or decades, like Pepsi or Coke—companies that sell virtually the same fizzy sugar water?

Solve Customers' Problems, Not Yours

So, you started your business. Got all your ducks in a row. Did the market research. Decided how much to charge. And you have done your financial projections. You know you have a good product and with your margins, you expect to make a killing.

Then reality sinks in.

Sales are lagging. People just aren't appreciating the value of your products or services. That is so frustrating. Why can't people see the value of what your company offers?

Simple answer. Everything above—every sentence, every word, every syllable is JUST ABOUT YOU. Without putting too fine a point on it, customers don't give a rat's keister about your success, or how you lovingly hand-made the product while wearing your fingers down to nibs.

Think about it. When you buy a car, for example, does GM's or Ford's or BMW's or Nissan's quarterly report showing their margins down 1.8 percent matter to you? Right. Well, your bottom line makes not one whit of difference to your customers.

This thinking leads directly to the quicksand, do not pass go, do not collect $200. You are stuck because you are not thinking about solving other people's problems, only your own.

You need to tell customers what you can do for them, not what they can do for you.

The mantra for developing a product, service, marketing approach, must originate from the client/consumer's perspective.

A few years ago, I was called in to help with a cable/mobility/Internet company. They had some success in launching their company against the established brands. However, their strategy was, unfortunately, based solely on price.

The content providers (my clients' suppliers) were all about to raise their prices, putting my clients' entire business strategy at risk. They were afraid that when they told their customers about price increases, it would result in an exodus of their current customers.

Buried deep in their panic, my client missed the key phrase: the content providers, not my client, were responsible for the price hike.

I put forward this crazy idea that this was not a disaster in the making, but an incredible opportunity. The problem was not high prices. It was demonstrating value.

We took clear aim at the content providers for raising their prices yet again, while showing customers that our client was the abused, not the abuser. Simultaneously, our client came to the rescue by absorbing these costs by offering bundles with deep discounts. It worked.

Workbook

1. Think of three occasions where you may have missed a sale, contract, or opportunity because you focused on you and not what the customer wanted or needed.
2. How would you have handled it differently?
3. Review the material on your website, literature, and any other place you plant your flag. Analyze how much of it speaks about you versus speaking to your prospective buyer/client's needs.
4. Fix it.

Don't Be Afraid to Ask

Timidity has no place in business. What's yours is yours, so ask. The very worst someone can say is "no," and that just means finding yet another way to ask.

The stuck entrepreneur is like a deer in the headlights. They freeze up in situations that call for action, especially when it involves asking for something. Even when they are entitled to ask and receive, they hesitate, and that includes asking for anything and everything. Here are examples of "asks" often camouflaged in hesitancy.

- An opportunity to meet face-to-face
- A chance to quote or bid
- A contract
- A security deposit/upfront payment
- An investment
- An accounts receivable that is due or past due (even when your creditors and suppliers are pursuing payment from you, kind of like what you ought to be doing with your customers)
- An invitation to participate in an event

...and the list goes on and on

Stuck entrepreneurs are not complacent, but likely have an inherent fear of rejection. Their anxiety of stepping into the quicksand, making a mistake, or imposing themselves precludes their ability to act or ask.

Does this describe you? Let's change that. There are fail-safe ways to ask for just about anything.

Firstly, let's differentiate "fearless" and "reckless."

- The **fearless** entrepreneur is not afraid to ask. They have hopes and expectations of being rewarded.
- The **reckless** entrepreneur punches way above their class in the belief, true or false, that they are simply entitled.

Be fearless, please.

I had a partner who "danced." He was a skilled communication-dodger, and attending meetings with him was excruciatingly painful. He dominated every discussion and talked endless small-talk. He did non-sensical conversational cartwheels that produced nothing. He never asked for anything. Even when I changed the direction of the meeting toward an "ask," he ratcheted it back to chitchat. Together, we accomplished nothing more than listening to him rave yet again about his favorite sports teams or boozy Mexican resorts. On my own, I was the deal closer.

Overcome your fear and hesitancy about asking. Here is how to do it.

- Don't think you asking will inconvenience anyone.
- Assume they expect you to ask, so don't disappoint them.
- Find a respected role model, and when confronted with an uncertain ask moment, think about what they would do or say.
- Imagine the result if you don't ask, for yourself and for your business. Focus on the outcome of asking.
- Be a leader who acknowledges fear but moves beyond it anyways.
- Don't take business rejection personally.
- Have confidence that what you are offering is what the customer or market needs and wants.
- Be self-assured in your own convictions, your ability to ask, and accept the outcomes.
- Prepare yourself for hearing "no" with alternatives. Always have a fallback "Plan B."
- Don't confuse a business relationship with a personal one. You must not assume asking for a business commitment can jeopardize the relationship. These are two distinct worlds.
- Work on your timing. Don't ask until you clearly identify that the other party has bought into what you are about to ask for. Listen for the verbal clues and watch their body language.

This approach is a mindset that applies to everything and everyone in business.

- Your people, your team
- Your personal and professional relationships
- Existing customers
- Would-be clients
- Those you network with, including lead generators/multipliers who refer business to you

Remember that you are the asker, and the other party is the askee (think we just made up a new word, but it works!).

- If the askee responds with "yes," just stop asking. The deed is done.
- If the askee says "no," find out why. What could you do or offer to make them accept your ask?
- If the askee says "maybe," find out when is the right time and what is the possible hesitation you need to overcome. Set a deal-closing Action Plan.

My mother always used to tell me "If you don't ask, you won't get. So, ask!" Mom was wise.

Workbook

1. List five characteristics you have that might qualify you as a stuck entrepreneur when it comes to asking for what you want or deserve.
   - Can you change any of these? How?
2. Think of five times you delivered an "ask" and were rewarded.
   - What did you do right? Was it timing? Content? Something else?
   - Document it so that you can repeat it again in the future.
3. Let's do the reverse now. Think of five times you delivered an "ask" and were snubbed.
   - What did you do wrong?
   - Document it so that you never repeat it again in the future.
4. Create an "ask" for any situation you chose where the askee cannot say no.
   - Test it out.

Getting Out of a Malignant Partnership

Best advice? Don't get into a partnership.

Yes, I understand. It was the excitement of having tapped into a sugar daddy (or momma). No more money worries, at least not for now. A mountain of new promised connections. Wow! A veritable shortcut to the next growth cycle of your venture without the normal growing pains. Wow again! What can possibly go wrong with this dream-like scenario?

Lots, and it often does, leaving you grasping for an exit from someone who is likely richer, better connected, and more powerful than you are. After all, money and markets are likely the main reasons you took the conjugal leap.

I once found a partner with great ideas. He was clever, well-spoken, and enthusiastic. I did not (or would not) recognize that his constant ramblings were part of a manic personality disorder exacerbated by recreational pharmaceuticals. The partnership always revolved around his brainstorms and my money, but I soon quashed this one-sided relationship by refusing to be the bank.

We subsequently fought incessantly, and I should have terminated the relationship as soon as his berserk behavior percolated at every get-together. Human nature often spawns hesitation at the wrong times.

One day, for some bizarro reason, he launched into a personal, vicious tirade against my young son for sitting in his spot on my couch. It was cruel and unforgivable. It was my trigger to end it all, but I had waited too long. I was stuck. The split was costly and upsetting.

In earlier, less antagonistic times, he had admitted that, when he was dead and gone, he wanted his ashes spread over the coastal waterway channel near our home. On the very day that I ended our business relationship, I magnanimously offered "Why wait? Let's do it today."

When the love is gone, the fangs and claws come out.

Here are some red flag indicators that the partnership has stepped off the yellow brick road.

- Partners lose steam and stop contributing their time, ideas, or resources to the company.
- They become distracted with other projects and opportunities; other shiny coins on the road.
- There is little depth in anything they do undertake, and the deliverables remain undelivered.
- Spending money to grow the business is often voted down or trimmed to marginal levels.
- They hire a new assistant who has few duties in your company, but who does become your partners' shadow.
- Secrecy becomes part of your partner's behavior.
- They try to freeze you out of important aspects of the business such as budgeting, capital expenditures, and hiring/firing.
- The "blame game" becomes a mainstay of your interactions. You get the blame for everything that goes wrong, and conversely, they are always the hero for the victories.
- Skipping key meetings (or leaving meetings early) becomes part of their irrational conduct.
- Their demeanor changes. You are perceived by them as a roadblock to other opportunities and the resentment is more than just a nagging feeling.
- Any efforts to discuss solutions or burgeoning difficulties with them are rebuffed.

I am assuming at this point that you have waited too long to act to disintegrate the partnership, and you are now stuck. Here are some action items you can take.

- Journalize everything; every argument, every unpartner-like behavior they may act out.
- Establish a clear division of responsibility and track performance, yours and theirs.
- Chances are your partner has deeper pockets. You need to counter that by having a "bully hand." That is, a street fighter

lawyer who is not intimidated by someone's balance sheet or power network. Their role is to defend you and together you need to create a "Plan B," in case problems arise. Find someone who also scares you. That is a prerequisite.

- Never let your partners' lawyer draft the Partnership or Dissolution Agreement. It should be done between both parties' lawyers.
- Watch out for the winding down of the honeymoon, the dangerous period when "love conquers all" gets conquered. When it fades and loses its lustrous sheen, problems and inequity can set in. Falling out of love can result in a hard landing.
- Get to know your partner. Find a weakness you can exploit later if necessary.
- Document any efforts to negotiate a buyout.
- As well, document any of their behavior that is irrational, or damaging to the company. This all becomes fodder later on if and when the tug of war ensues.

The easiest route is to buy them out. The less they have to do with the day-to-day business operations, the stronger your position and the less you need to offer since they cannot run the business on their own.

The objectives of amicability and fairness, in my experience, are in short supply the longer you take to act. Prolonged infighting is deadly. Even if you win, you may be mentally exhausted or be too dispirited to carry on.

The lessons here are simple. Prepare. Be cautious. Acknowledge the risks.

1. Do your homework before you go into any relationship that locks you down. Check out the prospective partner. Find out who they may have partnered with before, and speak with them.
2. Create a quantifiable division of responsibility and deliverables for each party, and track them continuously.
3. Wherever possible, enter a honeymoon period of working together before you jump into the sack. Once your partnership is consummated, there are so many other legal and binding factors that enter into the play. And the "stuck factor" can become a burden.

If this almost sounds like actually getting married, it is, but a business divorce can be tougher and can be more painful to extricate yourself from when both parties dig their heels and egos in.

However, if envisioning a business partnership like a personal marriage helps you visualize the potential risks and downfalls, then picture your business partner as your betrothed, but possibly with sharper claws, and fewer scruples.

Workbook

If you are thinking of **going into a partnership**, this exercise is for you.

1. Construct a profile of your ideal business partner.
2. What would you want them to bring to the table?
3. How would you split the areas of responsibility?
4. If you have someone in mind, have you carried out a backgrounder check and are you content with the results?
5. Do you share the same goals, ethics, and values? Go heavy on the "ethics."

If you are **already in a partnership**, this exercise is for you.

1. Do you have a Partnership Agreement?
2. Are there escape clauses in there that would allow you to exit without extraordinary costs and pain?
3. Do you have a buyout clause? A shotgun buyout clause? Have you examined these models? If not, do so. Ask your lawyer.
4. Has your Agreement been reviewed by your own lawyer? Have you followed their expensive advice? Remember, they are on your team.
5. Have you ever had discussions with your partner about eventually going separate ways? You should, especially while love is still lingering in the air and neither of you can imagine business life without the other.
6. Was there a viable dissolution model agreed upon? If not, keep working on it. Use a third-party mediator if you need to.

The Joy of Reframing

One of the great opportunities that presents itself to stuck entrepreneurs is the opportunity to step back, to take some time and think about what is really important to you. You get the luxury of a pause. Time to take a deep breath and revisit your business desires and personal goals. In the world of stuck entrepreneurs, this is known as *reframing*. It is a gut-wrenching experience and there isn't enough Pepto-Bismol to make it easy, but it will pay off big time.

Reframing can be as simple as seeing things in a new way, a fresh start. The silver lining here is that you can escape the hamster wheel of everyday trappings that are holding you back.

Where to start?

Write your personal vision then break it down into short term doable pieces. If your vision is your long-term financial independence, for example, then your near-term goals could be getting three new key customers every few months.

In both your personal and business life, you can use reframing as a source of positive change. Numerous studies show that if you feel trapped or stuck, it's likely that the stories you have created for yourself reflect exactly that—stuck. You can actually reframe these images and establish a new and more successful course.

Here are some of the things that always seem to bubble to the surface when visions and goals are examined. They are part of the "what is really important to you" discussion.

Time. Time is the world's ultimate currency. You only have so much and you can't create more, so you really need to be aware of how you are using it. Think of *spending* your time/currency in your business in conjunction with and in balance with *investing* your time/currency in friends, family, and yourself. Somewhere there is a happy medium.

Money. Unfortunately, money always comes into the stuck equation. Chasing working capital is a *gotta do* for most stuck businesses but it is not the only money consideration. Just as important is for the entrepreneur to understand their own money goals. A simple proforma cash flow will help you determine your own goals and milestones and how it will affect your business and personal life.

Stress Management. Every entrepreneur faces the specter of becoming overwhelmed by the stress associated with being the lead goose in the flock. You are not alone, but you need to find that unique outlet, be it morning jogs, woodworking, sailing, or writing a book as therapy. Whatever it is, you need to make it part of your life.

Exit Plan. Having a clear image of what your exit plan may be will always help you with the day-to-day issues of a company that is struggling to establish itself and prosper. Having a clear image of where you want to go is always good.

Discipline. The main impediment to realizing a reframed plan is the discipline required to execute it. Most successful entrepreneurs have very specific plans that dedicate explicit blocks of time to both their business and personal goals. Discipline of time management issues offers you a sense of control in your life.

Workbook

1. Write your own vision statement. What do you really care about and where do you want to go? Dreams that include being ruler of the world or having Jeff Bezos's wealth might not work. Keep it simple, realistic, and personal.
2. If you could change any one thing in your life today what would it be?
   - How would you change it?
   - What difference will it make in your life?
   - Are you willing to take the necessary steps? Turn the opportunity into action?
3. List the personal and business goals that you hope to achieve in the next six months.
4. Now list your long-term goals. This is where you can go wild; you pick the length of the term and your goals.

A Quicksand Avoidance Technique

Let's have a look at a real-world test case involving a belligerent and obstinate past client. A self-made entrepreneur running a profitable business. *Good for them!* Someone who also relished the status quo in a changing market where the state of play was shifting. *Bad for them!*

The following represents an almost verbatim tense conversation I had with him. This typifies one of many. He was a slow learner.

Let's call him "Acme" and call me "Me." (Not very imaginative, I know, but this makes life easier for the representation below.)

Me: How is business?

Acme: Business is great. We are making terrific profits.

Me: Are your margins holding up?

Acme: Competition and foreign imports are biting into our margins, but, so far, they are still good.

Me: How about your product mix?

Acme: We have increased our lines to offer even more to our clients and to keep imports at bay.

Me: Are you trimming old, slow moving inventory?

Acme: We will worry about that later.

Me: Hmmmm. Not sure about that. But let's look at your revenue climb.

Acme: It's stable.

Me: You mean more products but no increase in sales? I don't like that. It's a "quicksand trigger.

Acme: A what?

Me: A quicksand trigger. You know, the early signs that you might be heading for trouble. Better to avoid trouble than having to claw your way out of a hole.

Acme: Like what other triggers?

Me: Like several months of declining or stagnant revenues; sales primarily generated by only a small percentage of your products and services; more competition coming on stream; falling unit prices; and the need to increase discounts to maintain your customer base. These are a few Quicksand Triggers.

Acme: And if I don't pay attention?

Me: Dead stock. Inventory write downs. Cash flow shortfalls. Bank reporting problems. Customer drift.

Acme: What?

Me: With quicksand, once you're deep into it, there's no sink-or-swim. It's sink.

Acme: What do we do to avoid this?

Me: "The Quicksand Avoidance Chart

At that point, I presented what I felt was a valuable planning tool that I am now sharing with you in the following Workbook pages.

Workbook

There are two Planning tools, actually; one for your business, and one for you, the entrepreneur/businessperson.

The Business Quicksand Avoidance Chart

Using this format, create a chart for each sector of your business that should be tracked. Choose the ones that have previously, or can likely in the future, impact you dramatically enough to draw you toward an unpleasant (and possibly unexpected trip) to the quicksand pit.

These sectors can include but are not necessarily limited to any of the following: growth, operations, human resources, sales force, budgets versus actual variances review, funded/investor communications; competition, industry trends; industry forecasts; market shifts; client profiles; cash flow needs and resources available; financial performance; key ratios (for example, annual inventory turnover, and balance sheet changes/acid test, to mention a few). Include sectors that you generally don't like to deal with. Sectors you normally let slide.

This undertaking will take time to compile, and needs to be done by you in a quiet place, outside the distractions of the day-to-day workplace. Reflect, be honest with yourself, and judicious in your observations.

Once created, these charts will become action-item-oriented yardsticks. They will certainly help you build greater awareness for the direction (and possible misdirections) of your company.

So, jump right in. No general, go-nowhere stuff. No fatal "I won't think about this now" excuses. No pointless fluff. And, once completed, set a follow-up schedule to regularly review and update your Quicksand Avoidance Chart masterpiece.

The business Quicksand Avoidance Chart

Sector:	Details:
Identified pending issues. Immediate action required. Now!	
Medium term issues. Awareness and tracking are key.	
Longer term issues, including larger scale impactful events likely to transpire downstream, that is, regulatory issues, threats over which you have little or no control, and so on.	
What are the triggers for each identified item?	
When is corrective and proactive action required?	
What doable and affordable mitigating strategies can and should be considered?	
Action taken? Outcomes?	
Lessons learned for next time around?	

The Personal Quicksand Avoidance Chart

Personal issues impact business, and an entrepreneurs' ability to act. More importantly, business stuff seems to be of far lesser importance when you have stressful personal baggage that, most often, cries for some short-term attention.

Facing personal issues can be difficult. Nobody really likes to acknowledge their flaws and shortcomings. But personal issues can cloud the process that helps you evade business quicksand dangers. They often force us to delay action, which can be just as deadly.

So, use this suggested format to create a Personal Quicksand Avoidance Trigger Chart and run it alongside its business cousin discussed earlier.

Personal category	Issue identified	Action required	Deadline	Done?
Stress and anxiety				
Social and cultural issues				
Family/relationships				
Financial pressures				
Time constraints				
Overwhelming responsibilities				
Personal feelings of deprivation				
Other life priorities				
Change of personal focus				
Changing risk level tolerance				
Physical health issues				
Conflicts with other opportunities that have surfaced				

It is worth noting that these Quicksand Avoidance Charts don't resolve problems for you, but they can give you the impetus to face and deal with issues, challenges, and opportunities for bettering your business, and equipping you as your company's "motivational, involved leader."

More Personal Quicksand (Mis)Adventures

It's human nature to sometimes jump in when we should be tiptoeing around the edge, or when circumstances place us in a situation that is so haplessly absurd that our only response is to ride it out and to try to enjoy the adventure. Business is no different.

These business adventures, and misadventures, while often hilarious in hindsight, offer up invaluable lessons of what to do, or not do ever again. We learn and move on; all the wiser for how to avoid the quicksand.

Nobody Loves You When You're Nobody

When I retired, for the second time, having just sold my "final" business, I was extolled as a hero by my young staff. I paid off all their student loans and even helped them buy new toys.

There was a good-bye party arranged, glowing testimonials delivered, gifts of thanks, and a strong message of "we need to stay in touch" delivered. I was touched by this outpouring.

My expectation was that I would be the "grand sage" whose guidance and advice would be sought regularly. I relished the envisioned role, and even looked forward to hearing all the gossip of who was doing who, what new contracts were in the pipeline and how people were having difficulties without me there. How's that for an egotistical pipedream?

The reality was far simpler. Nothing happened. Stillness prevailed. No real follow-up except from my former Administrative Assistant, but that only lasted a few weeks. Other than that, no followers, no fan club, no advice sought, no problems asking to be solved. Nothing. Everyone simply moved on without me.

Gone is gone. When you are active and involved, your role can be god-like. But once you have left the building, you are on your own.

Business acquaintances are only friends when you are useful to them. Business can be fickle that way.

People Are Greedy

On behalf of a client, I pitched a supermarket shopping app at a Las Vegas investment forum. The offering was "the real deal." The company had revenues, new contracts in place, and a product that was temporarily disruptive. I use the term "temporarily" because, as you know, technology gets leapfrogged faster than your new cellphone being replaced often by five newer, improved models. But, at that moment, it was the leader.

The pitch went well. The audience reaction was lukewarm at best, which, in hindsight, was not terribly surprising. After all, this was Vegas; gamblers paradise. Win big or go home, right?

The next presentation was a stunner. An old, craggy cowboy prospector, decked out in a wide-brim snakeskin Stetson and weighed down with enough silver buckles and bling that jingled and clanged as he moved about, took the stage. The audience woke up.

Before him was a photo of a large hill with the title Gold Mountain. Just a freakin' hill in the middle of nowhere, really. He offered up some history of Gold Rush Days and old assay reports when gold was extracted from the mountain decades ago. Nothing current, though.

Pictures of gold nuggets flashed across the screen. The investor audience stirred some more.

One investor asked "How do you know there's still gold there?" The response was "How do you know there's not?" That was good enough for the audience. More impatient shuffling.

When the presenter offered the opportunity for interested parties to come up on stage and buy a piece of the dream, it was like a massive church communion rush. Checkbooks in hand, investors jockeyed for position on the staircase leading up to the stage. The chaos was laughable.

The secret was hitting the right hot buttons for the right audience at the right venue. That was a great lesson I learned, and guides me personally every time I present today. And I still hear that old cowboy jingling and clanging in the background. He knew.

Sometimes You Just Need to Jump In

Not everything in business demands careful planning and scrutiny. It should, actually, but sometimes it feels right to just jump into the deep end of the pool. The OMG factor is exhilarating.

That's what happened to me, and it was the conflux of two forces approaching me simultaneously but independently; an invitation from a Shanghai media contact to find a North American outdoors adventure program for their network of five hundred million viewers, and a call from a popular and bigger-than-life nature TV series star looking for alternate opportunities.

The stars were aligned. I just had to be the conduit.

Along the way, I learned about the intricacies of negotiating a broadcast license, especially in an overseas communist market. Once my scars began to heal, I conscripted the talent to help me.

I adapted to a culture steeped in traditional and fixated customs and regulations. I had to unlearn the ways of our relaxed North American standards of communication, networking, and doing business. Guanxi, the Chinese art of exchanging business favors (and lies) became my new standard operating model.

This amazing experience lasted two years and included a number of trips to China. I stumbled my way with Mr. Fan (pseudonym), the Assistant to the Assistant Director of the Peoples Republic of China (PRC) censorship arm (actually the Party Central Propaganda Department and General Administration of Radio, Film and Television). We became quite friendly. He lectured me about deleting phrases like "Oh My God" from my series (no religion allowed!) and I rattled his chains about them allowing Baywatch to air in China. Apparently, T&A is more acceptable than proliferating religion.

I often reflected how a fast-moving tadpole, such as myself, managed to survive and even flourish in a huge pond filled with tadpole-munching predators, such as everyone else around me back then.

The exhilaration of learning as you go is majestic, albeit sometimes bewildering. It made me a stronger, more confident entrepreneur, but also taught me to limit my extravagant business risk-taking. I was fortunate this time, but did not want to ruin my run of luck.

A Business Model Based on Elastic
Business Ethics

In my formative years, I worked for a conglomerate as Group Controller/ Director of Business Development. A lot of title for not a great deal of money. I was told by my employer that titles were handed out much freer than salary bumps. But I digress.

One of the companies under my charge was a bulk propane distribution operation. I paid very little attention to it because it seemed to just chug along at its own pace, shipping railcars filled with propane from one refinery to a small handful of redistributors. Always the same single supplier and always the same few buyers. Payment to the supplier and collection for shipments to customers ran like clockwork. It was a cash cow.

Any discussions I initiated to expand this successful business model was met with a firm "NO. LEAVE IT ALL ALONE AS IS."

Coincidence #1. Curiosity got the better of me. I dug for details and discovered that a higher up at the huge propane supply company was good friends with the owner of our own company.

Coincidence #2. Our contact at the huge propane supplier agreed to refuse credit to a number of smaller (but still pretty significant) redistribution companies who were, by no coincidence, the only customers we sold to.

This went on during my entire tenure at the company. Big Boy refused to sell to Little Guy, but we would not hesitate to pick up those rejected accounts. It was business incest at its finest.

This lasted until our connection at the large-scale supplier retired. His replacement changed credit-granting policies, and our middleman status evaporated instantly.

The lesson? Not all businesses are based on earth-shattering technology or bleeding-edge disruptive strategies. Some are just based on the simplest of things, like an understanding between old friends, and inserting yourself where others cannot or would not tread.

And who was I to differentiate between possible collusion and advantageous coincidence? Elastic business ethics, right?

I Know Everything

It's not true, obviously. I am not quite than vain. However, I know enough to join into most conversations. I am a master at knowing a little about a lot. That's the beauty of working with so many different clients across a wide economic spectrum over a number of years.

But there are people who profess universal knowledge. Touch on any subject and they can spout endless numbers, trends, the latest events, and just about any relevant (and irrelevant) piece of information. Impressive, but are they telling you the truth? I assume there are gaps.

I have made a game of picking holes in what I hear told. Just at the right time, at the right spot in a conversation, I will drop a fact that questions the veracity of what I am hearing. It doesn't take much.

It's kind of entertaining watching someone hesitate, backpedal, and deal with this unexpected mini-confrontation. The haughtier the know-it-all, the greater enjoyment watching them react. The process also created a greater awareness of me amongst my peers.

This strategy effectively levels out the interaction playing field. Then the communication really begins.

On Emulating a Business Rebel

I zeroed in on this one guy who seemed to show up everywhere I did at all the conferences and networking sessions. What caught my attention was his style and demeanor.

He was always dressed trendy casual. Never a suit. Often jeans, open white shirt, casual sports jacket, and flamboyant runners. No pinkie rings or pimp gold chains. He carried himself like he didn't really care about much, well, maybe just enough to join group conversations of his choosing, moreso as an observer.

His smile was warm and genuine, and he was a toucher; shoulder taps, double handshakes, the occasional hug, you know the kind. He knew he was swoon-worthy to both sexes.

He was not someone of any great consequence, position, or wealth, but you wouldn't know it by the crowds he attracted. Real people, not the usual hangers-on. It was like he was emitting behavior-altering pheromones. It was magic to watch.

Slowly, I began to emulate him, adopting his style, dress, aloofness, physicality, and attitude. But mostly his temperament. It was a major transition for me coming from the more traditional sheep-like school of fitting in, but it worked.

I developed a reputation as the square peg in a round hole; someone who knew something, and someone worth knowing.

I relished my new "go to" status and still do.

Impress the Lowest Common Denominator

I have sat through my share, and then some, of presentations designed to inform, impress, and solicit investment and support. Most were well-packaged but aimed too high.

The assumption seems to be that everyone listening has a certain level of knowledge, awareness of the company, the project, the sector, and the area of opportunity. That is not the case in any reasonable-sized audience, and especially not true in a larger setting.

Presentations require two objectives: (1) deliver a clear and understandable message of what you are trying to say, and what the "ask" is, and (2) connect with the audience. As far as the latter goes, I have often been forced to stretch my knowledge to try to comprehend what has gotten the presenter so excited about, and why I should likewise be intrigued and enthralled.

In too many cases, it just does not come off right. This is true moreso if the opportunities are in the fields of technology, biotech, pharmaceutical, medical, Internet security, or a host of other sectors that are, apparently, ones I am only peripherally familiar with.

I am reminded of one particular investor pitch that I had to interrupt midstream after 20 minutes of their dog-and-pony show and inquire exactly what their company did. By that time, however, they had made me aware of how experienced and educated their team was, which was done to impress (and possibly intimidate), but did not really help me to comprehend their technology.

I was actually there with an investor friend, very well-to-do, but not terribly tech-savvy. He walked out mid-stream, professing that he was probably too dumb to invest in this when, in fact, he could have funded the entire project had they not insulted him by pitching way, way over his head.

When I am scheduled to pitch, I try to find out who will be in the audience, large or small. I then gear my presentation at a lower or mid-level to assure my message gets through to almost everyone. And I watch body language. If I see uncomfortable jitters anywhere in the group, I step it down, or just stop for questions. I won't forego my, or my clients' opportunities by limiting audience buy-in. I try not to repeat others' mistakes.

I Am Appalled by Echinoderms, Mollusks, and Giant Digging Clams

I am disgusted by sea cucumbers, and the oxymoron "edible sea cucumber" makes me gag. I have the same reaction to even imaging "edible" slugs, snails, urchins, sea stars, and geoducks. I have never accepted how these lowly, ugly creatures have become costly delicacies, sought out, and worshipped by certain cultures.

I still remember going to the beach as a child and being warned by my mother "Don't step on any of those squishy or pointy things." Today I see them on restaurant menus, and on the expensive side of the menus at that, and my mother's warning still haunts me.

And yet, in business, we accommodate. We do things we might never think of doing in "real life," like eating a detested echinoderm (I cannot even bring myself to say "sea cucumber") to impress a client.

That is the one horrific occasion that comes to mind. China's largest sea cucumber producer was interested in my client's technology to grow these monstrosities to an even larger size. He hosted an evening where he served up steamed (yes, you heard it right) sea cucumbers to us all.

We partook in this feast, proclaiming our appreciation for the gourmet opportunity and to congratulate the Chinese producer for his ability to prepare these atrocities in a way that they retained all, I repeat, all of their (hideous) subtleties.

In the end, the deal to license the technology did not materialize. I was truly upset that I ate these echinoderms without reaping any rewards. If the deal was done, would I have felt less sick?

Apparently, business imposes few limits on our personal values, at least on mine.

Never Settle for "Carrots"

I always believed that it was true when I was promised more, even bigger contracts in the future, if cut my prices on this one. It was often just non-sense. A cheap negotiation trick.

Inevitably, the "carrot on the stick" was an illusion, a ploy. This was not always the case, but far too often it was a game in which the outcome was stacked against me.

Naivety is a cruel teacher. It took me a while to fully appreciate how people take advantage of each other. I needed to develop a counterplan.

I sought the upper hand. I took a stand. My pitch was basically and consistently as follows:

1. Our company delivers results.
2. We offer fair pricing that is not open to negotiation.
3. We expect you will engage us downstream for more work. When that happens, we will offer an xx percent thank you discount, but it only applies on the next contract, not on this one.
4. If you are fixated on price, I can send you some competitors who work for less. But please understand that if we take on work to clean others' mess, our costs to you will actually be far higher.

What amazed me was that this approach worked. The same people who try to take advantage of you also respect you when you show some backbone.

What's in a Name?

Once a startup junkie, always a start-up junkie.

In between launching two of my ventures, I decided to get involved in the outdoors tourism sector. Being fond of canoeing, kayaking, fishing, hiking, whale watching, and exploring, I launched an outdoors adventure company. It was basically a booking agency. My objectives were twofold: (1) I could spend time outdoors, and more deviously (2) in order to recommend any number of remote resorts to my international client base, I needed to visit and review the facilities. This meant freebie invitations and trips to the finest retreats. As I said, "devious."

My business was called "The Outdoors Adventure Company." It was successful, but limited in size and scope. Growth was barely marginal. My startup junkie genes encouraged me to run this like a real business instead of a hobby. I recognized that I needed a greater presence in the marketplace, a stronger brand identity.

Aside from developing a more diverse content marketing strategy, I decided to change the name of the business to "The World's Greatest Outdoor Adventure Company." This was pure hype, but the impact was amazing.

Trip travel agents/distributors from overseas began to court me. Nature resorts who had previously ignored me were now inviting me (again, free) to visit. Regional airlines who flew into these resorts wanted to joint market with me. It became a real business!

Was it the name change? Partly. But the new identity gave me the ability to upscale my entire family of products, and obviously helped hit the mark with both customers and suppliers.

Sex Still Sells, But It's Different Now

At the last pre-Covid trade show I attended, there was the usual flourish, hype, and excitement at exhibitor booths. To my great surprise, there was one booth that still used scantily-clad models as spokespeople. I was intrigued to watch the crowds, mostly men, gather around and gawk. I was in disbelief that this archaic, sexist approach was still used to capture and captivate the crowd.

Then, I just started to listen, really listen to the ongoing dialogue. I noticed something interesting. These women were exceptionally smart. They knew everything about the exhibitor's products and responded succinctly to any questions thrown their way. These spokeswomen could easily have been part of the company's senior marketing team or certainly should have been.

The interaction between these women and the onlookers was quite professional and very respectful. The few gawkers faded away pretty quickly.

While I did not approve of the strategy, I realized we have entered a new age of respect in marketing. It might be okay to use beautiful people, as long as you don't use beautiful hollow-shell people. This rejigged stereotype throws the audience/viewership off balance, and they pay attention. Convention be damned.

That Monkey on Your Back Is Called Greed

Greed is the crack-cocaine of business. It implies seeking out greater wealth and power than a person needs (or likely deserves), and is often harmful to other folks who get in the way. It is careless, callous, and, unfortunately, also imbedded into the DNA of who we are as business people.

It can tempt us to act way outside our comfort zone for an improbable reward dangled in front of our nose. It often encourages us to misbehave, but it can also teach us to respect limits.

Meet Quentin, the financial hustler. His pitch was to take my company public, and cash in on a strong investor market. The idea made sense, but Quentin didn't quite add up.

The more we worked together, the more I woke sweating in the night. Quentin's history didn't quite check out, and his references were semi-literate at best. But the glow of pending wealth kept me in the game, albeit uneasily.

One day, as I reviewed the documents to be filed with the investment brokerage firm, I noticed my signature on forms I had never seen, or signed. My signature was on each one, but they were completely identical, flaws and all. I woke up. I destroyed the documents and informed all parties that the filing was terminated.

Everyone needs a lesson in greed in order to set their personal framework of judging good versus abhorrent. Greed can distort those boundaries.

Since that day, I have rarely if ever fallen under the spell of blinding greed. I follow a simple principle: if it feels like a "Quentin," it's too good to be true.

Walk away before greed overrides reason.

Falling Asleep During a Zoom Call

I have to admit that, on occasion, and only in a larger group setting where I can substitute my live video feed for say, a photo of an adorable puppy, I sometimes nod off. It also speaks to my super power to catch a brief nap anytime, anywhere.

It is not out of any disrespect for the presenter(s), or the possibly inane subject matter. These are get-togethers I chose to attend, or needed to demonstrate my presence, albeit not my direct and active participation. I just needed to have my name on the attendees guest list.

In my defense, many of these events were snooze-fests; weak presenters spouting subject matter that attendees were already well aware of. Speaking down to your audience is a sure-fire way to lose them.

In my defense, my repose was never detected. I am a very light sleeper, and if and when my name was called out, I would spring to attention with responses like "Let's dive deeper into that" or "I'm still thinking about that. Let's talk more. Anybody else have any thoughts?"

Joking aside, these sessions were extremely useful. They taught me how, as a presenter, I can hold peoples' interest and participation. Make these Zooms (and webinars) highly interactive, add humor, show I am human, be a tad outrageous, even rebellious, and, most importantly, deliver something useful to the participants; make others feel important for being there, for giving up their time to contribute, speak, and add value.

And if you, as a webinar presenter, call upon someone to comment and you hear "Let me reflect on that" or "I'm not sure," you know you have lost them.

Especially if their video feed has been replaced by a cuddly puppy.

About the Author

Jay J. Silverberg is a "business rebel" who has started and run a number of successful businesses. This book is based on his business adventures (and misadventures) and offers up a multitude of inestimably valuable lessons. As an entrepreneurial trainer, Jay has developed innovative programs for both the beginner and the advanced businessperson, and delivered training and mentoring to thousands of entrepreneurs, managers, and business professionals.

As a business consultant, Jay's practice ranges from start-ups to Fortune 500 firms with projects that have spanned the globe. He has also represented government trade and economic development ministries at national and international conferences.

Jay Silverberg currently teaches various levels of entrepreneurship, and delivers business coaching and mentoring.

Jay resides in Vancouver, British Columbia, Canada with his wife, Linda, who inspires him to always see life as a gift, and business as a game (and vice versa). Jay can be contacted at silverberg88@gmail.com.

Previous Works

A Business Cynic's Wisdom: Winning Through Flexible Ethics, Business Expert Press, Oct/20 (Jay J. Silverberg, Author)

Dead Fish Don't Swim Upstream: Real Life Lessons in Entrepreneurship, Business Expert Press, November, 2021 (Jay J. Silverberg and Bruce E. McLean, co-authors)

Index

OTHER TITLES IN THE ENTREPRENEURSHIP AND SMALL BUSINESS MANAGEMENT COLLECTION

Scott Shane, Case Western University, Editor

- *Teaching Old Dogs New Tricks* by Thomas Waters
- *Building Business Capacity* by Sheryl Hardin
- *The Entrepreneurial Adventure* by Oliver James
- *So, You Bought a Franchise. Now What?* by David Roemer
- *The Startup Masterplan* by Nikhil Agarwal and Krishiv Agarwal
- *Managing Health and Safety in a Small Business* by Jacqueline Jeynes
- *Modern Devil's Advocacy* by Robert Koshinskie
- *Dead Fish Don't Swim Upstream* by Jay J. Silverberg and Bruce E. McLean
- *Founders, Freelancers & Rebels* by Helen Jane Campbell
- *The 8 Superpowers of Successful Entrepreneurs* by Marina Nicholas
- *Navigating the New Normal* by Rodd Mann
- *Time Management for Unicorns* by Giulio D'Agostino
- *Zero to $10 Million* by Shane Brett
- *Ethical Business Culture* by Andreas Karaoulanis
- *Blockchain Value* by Olga V. Mack

Concise and Applied Business Books

The Collection listed above is one of 30 business subject collections that Business Expert Press has grown to make BEP a premiere publisher of print and digital books. Our concise and applied books are for...

- Professionals and Practitioners
- Faculty who adopt our books for courses
- Librarians who know that BEP's Digital Libraries are a unique way to offer students ebooks to download, not restricted with any digital rights management
- Executive Training Course Leaders
- Business Seminar Organizers

Business Expert Press books are for anyone who needs to dig deeper on business ideas, goals, and solutions to everyday problems. Whether one print book, one ebook, or buying a digital library of 110 ebooks, we remain the affordable and smart way to be business smart. For more information, please visit www.businessexpertpress.com, or contact sales@businessexpertpress.com.